MACBETH

WILLIAM SHAKESPEARE

FP CLASSICS

Published 2025

FiNGERPRINT! CLASSICS
Prakash Books

Fingerprint Publishing
@FingerprintP
@fingerprintpublishingbooks
www.fingerprintpublishing.com

ISBN: 978 81 7599 419 5

William Shakespeare began his career as an actor, writer, and part owner of a playing company called the Lord Chamberlain's Men, later known as King's Men, in London. Often regarded as the 'Bard of Avon' he is one of the world's pre-eminent dramatists. Born and brought up in Stratford-upon-Avon, he married Anne Hathaway at the age of eighteen and they had three children—Susanna, and twins Hamnet and Judith. Though few records survive of his private life, he appeared to have retired to Stratford around 1613 where he died three years later.

His works still in existence, including some collaborations, consist of thirty-eight plays, one hundred and fifty-four sonnets, two long narrative poems, and several other verses. His plays are performed much more than any other playwright's and have been translated in almost all major languages. Most of his known works have been produced between 1589 and 1613. His early plays were mainly comedies and histories which remain regarded as some of the best works produced in these genres.

Shakespeare's plays are difficult to date. His early classical and Italianate comedies contain tight double plots and precise comic sequences giving way to the romantic atmosphere of his most acclaimed comedies in the mid-1590s. *A Midsummer Night's Dream*—a witty mixture of romance, fairy magic, and comic low life scenes—is one of his most delightful creations shortly before he turned to *Romeo and Juliet. Romeo and Juliet* is his most famous romantic tragedy of sexually charged adolescence, love, and death. It marks a departure from his earlier works and from others of the English Renaissance.

His plays demonstrate the expansiveness of his imagination and the extent of his learning. Shakespeare's sequence of great comedies continues with *Merchant of Venice*, *Much Ado About Nothing*, *As You Like It*, and *Twelfth Night*. He introduced prose comedy in the histories of the late 1590s—*Henry IV*, *Part I* and *Part II*, and *Henry V*—after the lyrical *Richard II*. *Julius Caesar* introduced a new kind of drama.

Shakespeare wrote the so-called 'problem plays' in the early 17th century. *Measure for Measure*, *Troilus and Cressida*, and *All's Well that Ends Well* being a few of them. Until about 1608, he mainly wrote tragedies including *Hamlet*, *Othello*, *King Lear*, and *Macbeth*. The story of a brave Scottish general named Macbeth, the eponymous drama illustrates how the lust for power dooms the fate of a noble person. When the trio of witches predict that Macbeth would eventually become the King of Scotland, his simmering ambitions overpower him, and persuaded by his wife he murders King Duncan and seizes the throne. But the play does not end here. In spite of being a man of guilt, he eventually becomes a tyrannical ruler. This Shakespearean tragedy has been adapted into multiple art forms across the centuries.

Antony and Cleopatra and *Coriolanus*—his last major tragedies, contain some of his finest poetry. Shakespeare wrote tragicomedies, also known as romances, in his last phase. These include *Cymbeline*, *The Winter's Tale*, and *The Tempest*, as well as the collaboration *Pericles, Prince of Tyre*.

A true genius, Shakespeare's popular characters and plots are studied, performed, reinterpreted, and discussed till today. William Shakespeare, known as the English national poet, is considered the greatest dramatist of all time.

Contents

Characters of the Play

DUNCAN, King of Scotland.

MACBETH, Thane of Glamis and Cawdor, a general in the King's army.

LADY MACBETH, his wife.

MACDUFF, Thane of Fife, a nobleman of Scotland.

LADY MACDUFF, his wife.

MALCOLM, elder son of Duncan.

DONALBAIN, younger son of Duncan.

BANQUO, Thane of Lochaber, a general in the King's army.

FLEANCE, his son.

LENNOX, ROSS, MENTEITH, ANGUS, CAITHNESS, noblemen of Scotland.

SIWARD, Earl of Northumberland, general of the English forces.

YOUNG SIWARD, his son.

SEYTON, attendant to Macbeth.

HECATE, Queen of the Witches.

Witches.

Boy, Son of Macduff.

Gentlewoman attending on Lady Macbeth.

An English Doctor.

A Scottish Doctor.

A Sergeant.

A Porter.

An Old Man.

The Ghost of Banquo and other Apparitions.

Lords, Gentlemen, Officers, Soldiers, Murtherers, Attendants, and Messengers.

Scene:
Scotland and England

ACT I

Scene I. A desert place.

Thunder and lightning. Enter three Witches

FIRST WITCH

When shall we three meet again
In thunder, lightning, or in rain?

SECOND WITCH

When the hurlyburly's done,
When the battle's lost and won.

THIRD WITCH

That will be ere the set of sun.

FIRST WITCH

Where the place?

SECOND WITCH

Upon the heath.

THIRD WITCH

There to meet with Macbeth.

FIRST WITCH

I come, Graymalkin!

SECOND WITCH

Paddock calls.

THIRD WITCH

Anon.

ALL

Fair is foul, and foul is fair:
Hover through the fog and filthy air.

Exeunt

Scene II. A camp near Forres.

Alarum within.

Enter Duncan, Malcolm, Donalbain, Lennox, with Attendants, meeting a bleeding Sergeant

DUNCAN

What bloody man is that? He can report,
As seemeth by his plight, of the revolt
The newest state.

MALCOLM

This is the sergeant
Who like a good and hardy soldier fought
'Gainst my captivity. Hail, brave friend!
Say to the king the knowledge of the broil
As thou didst leave it.

SERGEANT

Doubtful it stood;
As two spent swimmers, that do cling together
And choke their art. The merciless Macdonwald—

Worthy to be a rebel, for to that
The multiplying villanies of nature
Do swarm upon him—from the western isles
Of kerns and gallowglasses is supplied;
And fortune, on his damned quarrel smiling,
Show'd like a rebel's whore: but all's too weak:
For brave Macbeth—well he deserves that name—
Disdaining fortune, with his brandish'd steel,
Which smoked with bloody execution,
Like valour's minion carved out his passage
Till he faced the slave;
Which ne'er shook hands, nor bade farewell to him,
Till he unseam'd him from the nave to the chaps,
And fix'd his head upon our battlements.

DUNCAN

O valiant cousin! worthy gentleman!

SERGEANT

As whence the sun 'gins his reflection
Shipwrecking storms and direful thunders break,
So from that spring whence comfort seem'd to come
Discomfort swells. Mark, king of Scotland, mark:
No sooner justice had with valour arm'd
Compell'd these skipping kerns to trust their heels,
But the Norweyan lord surveying vantage,
With furbish'd arms and new supplies of men
Began a fresh assault.

DUNCAN

Dismay'd not this
Our captains, Macbeth and Banquo?

SERGEANT

Yes;
As sparrows eagles, or the hare the lion.
If I say sooth, I must report they were
As cannons overcharged with double cracks, so they
Doubly redoubled strokes upon the foe:
Except they meant to bathe in reeking wounds,
Or memorise another Golgotha,
I cannot tell.
But I am faint, my gashes cry for help.

DUNCAN

So well thy words become thee as thy wounds;
They smack of honour both. Go get him surgeons.

Exit Sergeant, attended

Who comes here?

Enter Ross

MALCOLM

The worthy thane of Ross.

LENNOX

What a haste looks through his eyes! So should he look
That seems to speak things strange.

ROSS

God save the king!

DUNCAN

Whence camest thou, worthy thane?

ROSS

From Fife, great king;
Where the Norweyan banners flout the sky
And fan our people cold. Norway himself,

With terrible numbers,
Assisted by that most disloyal traitor
The thane of Cawdor, began a dismal conflict;
Till that Bellona's bridegroom, lapp'd in proof,
Confronted him with self-comparisons,
Point against point rebellious, arm 'gainst arm.
Curbing his lavish spirit: and, to conclude,
The victory fell on us.

DUNCAN

Great happiness!

ROSS

That now
Sweno, the Norways' king, craves composition:
Nor would we deign him burial of his men
Till he disbursed at Saint Colme's inch
Ten thousand dollars to our general use.

DUNCAN

No more that thane of Cawdor shall deceive
Our bosom interest: go pronounce his present death,
And with his former title greet Macbeth.

ROSS

I'll see it done.

DUNCAN

What he hath lost noble Macbeth hath won.

Exeunt

Scene III. A heath near Forres.

Thunder. Enter the three Witches

FIRST WITCH

Where hast thou been, sister?

SECOND WITCH

Killing swine.

THIRD WITCH

Sister, where thou?

FIRST WITCH

A sailor's wife had chestnuts in her lap,
And munch'd, and munch'd, and munch'd:—
'Give me,' quoth I:
'Aroint thee, witch!' the rump-fed ronyon cries.
Her husband's to Aleppo gone, master o'the *Tiger*:
But in a sieve I'll thither sail,
And, like a rat without a tail,
I'll do, I'll do, and I'll do.

SECOND WITCH

I'll give thee a wind.

FIRST WITCH

Thou'rt kind.

THIRD WITCH

And I another.

FIRST WITCH

I myself have all the other,
And the very ports they blow,
All the quarters that they know
I'the shipman's card.
I will drain him dry as hay:

Sleep shall neither night nor day
Hang upon his pent-house lid;
He shall live a man forbid:
Weary se'nnights nine times nine
Shall he dwindle, peak and pine:
Though his bark cannot be lost,
Yet it shall be tempest-tost.
Look what I have.

SECOND WITCH

Show me, show me.

FIRST WITCH

Here I have a pilot's thumb,
Wreck'd as homeward he did come.

Drum within

THIRD WITCH

A drum, a drum!
Macbeth doth come.

ALL

The weird sisters, hand in hand,
Posters of the sea and land,
Thus do go about, about:
Thrice to thine and thrice to mine
And thrice again, to make up nine.
Peace! the charm's wound up.

Enter Macbeth and Banquo

MACBETH

So foul and fair a day I have not seen.

BANQUO

How far is't call'd to Forres? What are these

So wither'd and so wild in their attire,
That look not like the inhabitants o'the earth,
And yet are on't? Live you? or are you aught
That man may question? You seem to understand me,
By each at once her chappy finger laying
Upon her skinny lips: you should be women,
And yet your beards forbid me to interpret
That you are so.

MACBETH

Speak, if you can: what are you?

FIRST WITCH

All hail, Macbeth! hail to thee, thane of Glamis!

SECOND WITCH

All hail, Macbeth, hail to thee, thane of Cawdor!

THIRD WITCH

All hail, Macbeth, thou shalt be king hereafter!

BANQUO

Good sir, why do you start; and seem to fear
Things that do sound so fair? I'the name of truth,
Are ye fantastical, or that indeed
Which outwardly ye show? My noble partner
You greet with present grace and great prediction
Of noble having and of royal hope,
That he seems rapt withal: to me you speak not.
If you can look into the seeds of time,
And say which grain will grow and which will not,
Speak then to me, who neither beg nor fear
Your favours nor your hate.

FIRST WITCH

Hail!

SECOND WITCH

Hail!

THIRD WITCH

Hail!

FIRST WITCH

Lesser than Macbeth, and greater.

SECOND WITCH

Not so happy, yet much happier.

THIRD WITCH

Thou shalt get kings, though thou be none:
So all hail, Macbeth and Banquo!

FIRST WITCH

Banquo and Macbeth, all hail!

MACBETH

Stay, you imperfect speakers, tell me more:
By Sinel's death I know I am thane of Glamis;
But how of Cawdor? the thane of Cawdor lives,
A prosperous gentleman; and to be king
Stands not within the prospect of belief,
No more than to be Cawdor. Say from whence
You owe this strange intelligence? or why
Upon this blasted heath you stop our way
With such prophetic greeting? Speak, I charge you.

Witches vanish

BANQUO

The earth hath bubbles, as the water has,
And these are of them. Whither are they vanish'd?

MACBETH

Into the air; and what seem'd corporal melted
As breath into the wind. Would they had stay'd!

BANQUO

Were such things here as we do speak about?
Or have we eaten on the insane root
That takes the reason prisoner?

MACBETH

Your children shall be kings.

BANQUO

You shall be king.

MACBETH

And thane of Cawdor too: went it not so?

BANQUO

To the selfsame tune and words. Who's here?

Enter Ross and Angus

ROSS

The king hath happily received, Macbeth,
The news of thy success; and when he reads
Thy personal venture in the rebels' fight,
His wonders and his praises do contend
Which should be thine or his: silenced with that,
In viewing o'er the rest o'the selfsame day,
He finds thee in the stout Norweyan ranks,
Nothing afeard of what thyself didst make,
Strange images of death. As thick as hail
Came post with post; and every one did bear
Thy praises in his kingdom's great defence,
And pour'd them down before him.

ANGUS

We are sent
To give thee from our royal master thanks;
Only to herald thee into his sight,
Not pay thee.

ROSS

And, for an earnest of a greater honour,
He bade me, from him, call thee thane of Cawdor:
In which addition, hail, most worthy thane!
For it is thine.

BANQUO

What, can the devil speak true?

MACBETH

The thane of Cawdor lives: why do you dress me
In borrow'd robes?

ANGUS

Who was the thane lives yet;
But under heavy judgment bears that life
Which he deserves to lose. Whether he was combined
With those of Norway, or did line the rebel
With hidden help and vantage, or that with both
He labour'd in his country's wreck, I know not;
But treasons capital, confess'd and proved,
Have overthrown him.

MACBETH

[*Aside*] Glamis, and thane of Cawdor!
The greatest is behind.

To Ross and Angus

Thanks for your pains.

To Banquo

Do you not hope your children shall be kings,
When those that gave the thane of Cawdor to me
Promised no less to them?

BANQUO

That trusted home
Might yet enkindle you unto the crown,
Besides the thane of Cawdor. But 'tis strange:
And oftentimes, to win us to our harm,
The instruments of darkness tell us truths,
Win us with honest trifles, to betray's
In deepest consequence.
Cousins, a word, I pray you.

MACBETH

[*Aside*] Two truths are told,
As happy prologues to the swelling act
Of the imperial theme.—I thank you, gentlemen.
[*Aside*] This supernatural soliciting
Cannot be ill, cannot be good: if ill,
Why hath it given me earnest of success,
Commencing in a truth? I am thane of Cawdor:
If good, why do I yield to that suggestion
Whose horrid image doth unfix my hair
And make my seated heart knock at my ribs,
Against the use of nature? Present fears
Are less than horrible imaginings:
My thought, whose murder yet is but fantastical,
Shakes so my single state of man that function
Is smother'd in surmise, and nothing is

But what is not.

BANQUO

Look, how our partner's rapt.

MACBETH

[*Aside*] If chance will have me king, why, chance may crown
me,
Without my stir.

BANQUO

New horrors come upon him,
Like our strange garments, cleave not to their mould
But with the aid of use.

MACBETH

[*Aside*] Come what come may,
Time and the hour runs through the roughest day.

BANQUO

Worthy Macbeth, we stay upon your leisure.

MACBETH

Give me your favour: my dull brain was wrought
With things forgotten. Kind gentlemen, your pains
Are register'd where every day I turn
The leaf to read them. Let us toward the king.
Think upon what hath chanced, and, at more time,
The interim having weigh'd it, let us speak
Our free hearts each to other.

BANQUO

Very gladly.

MACBETH

Till then, enough. Come, friends.

Exeunt

Scene IV. Forres. The palace.

Flourish. Enter Duncan, Malcolm, Donalbain, Lennox, and Attendants

DUNCAN

Is execution done on Cawdor? Are not
Those in commission yet return'd?

MALCOLM

My liege,
They are not yet come back. But I have spoke
With one that saw him die: who did report
That very frankly he confess'd his treasons,
Implored your highness' pardon and set forth
A deep repentance: nothing in his life
Became him like the leaving it; he died
As one that had been studied in his death
To throw away the dearest thing he owed,
As 'twere a careless trifle.

DUNCAN

There's no art
To find the mind's construction in the face:
He was a gentleman on whom I built
An absolute trust.

Enter Macbeth, Banquo, Ross, and Angus

O worthiest cousin!
The sin of my ingratitude even now
Was heavy on me: thou art so far before
That swiftest wing of recompense is slow
To overtake thee. Would thou hadst less deserved,
That the proportion both of thanks and payment

Might have been mine! only I have left to say,
More is thy due than more than all can pay.

MACBETH

The service and the loyalty I owe,
In doing it, pays itself. Your highness' part
Is to receive our duties; and our duties
Are to your throne and state children and servants,
Which do but what they should, by doing every thing
Safe toward your love and honour.

DUNCAN

Welcome hither:
I have begun to plant thee, and will labour
To make thee full of growing. Noble Banquo,
That hast no less deserved, nor must be known
No less to have done so, let me enfold thee
And hold thee to my heart.

BANQUO

There if I grow,
The harvest is your own.

DUNCAN

My plenteous joys,
Wanton in fulness, seek to hide themselves
In drops of sorrow. Sons, kinsmen, thanes,
And you whose places are the nearest, know
We will establish our estate upon
Our eldest, Malcolm, whom we name hereafter
The Prince of Cumberland; which honour must
Not unaccompanied invest him only,
But signs of nobleness, like stars, shall shine

On all deservers. From hence to Inverness,
And bind us further to you.

MACBETH

The rest is labour, which is not used for you:
I'll be myself the harbinger and make joyful
The hearing of my wife with your approach;
So humbly take my leave.

DUNCAN

My worthy Cawdor!

MACBETH

[*Aside*] The Prince of Cumberland! that is a step
On which I must fall down, or else o'erleap,
For in my way it lies. Stars, hide your fires;
Let not light see my black and deep desires:
The eye wink at the hand; yet let that be,
Which the eye fears, when it is done, to see.

Exit

DUNCAN

True, worthy Banquo; he is full so valiant,
And in his commendations I am fed;
It is a banquet to me. Let's after him,
Whose care is gone before to bid us welcome:
It is a peerless kinsman.

Flourish. Exeunt

Scene V. Inverness. Macbeth's castle.

Enter Lady Macbeth, reading a letter

LADY MACBETH

'They met me in the day of success: and I have

learned by the perfectest report, they have more in them than mortal knowledge. When I burned in desire to question them further, they made themselves air, into which they vanished. Whiles I stood rapt in the wonder of it, came missives from the king, who all-hailed me "Thane of Cawdor;" by which title, before, these weird sisters saluted me, and referred me to the coming on of time, with "Hail, king that shalt be!" This have I thought good to deliver thee, my dearest partner of greatness, that thou mightst not lose the dues of rejoicing, by being ignorant of what greatness is promised thee. Lay it to thy heart, and farewell.'

Glamis thou art, and Cawdor; and shalt be
What thou art promised: yet do I fear thy nature;
It is too full o'the milk of human kindness
To catch the nearest way: thou wouldst be great;
Art not without ambition, but without
The illness should attend it: what thou wouldst highly,
That wouldst thou holily; wouldst not play false,
And yet wouldst wrongly win: thou'ldst have, great Glamis,
That which cries 'Thus thou must do, if thou have it;
And that which rather thou dost fear to do
Than wishest should be undone.' Hie thee hither,
That I may pour my spirits in thine ear;
And chastise with the valour of my tongue
All that impedes thee from the golden round,
Which fate and metaphysical aid doth seem
To have thee crown'd withal.

Enter a Messenger

What is your tidings?

MESSENGER

The king comes here to-night.

LADY MACBETH

Thou'rt mad to say it:
Is not thy master with him? who, were't so,
Would have inform'd for preparation.

MESSENGER

So please you, it is true: our thane is coming:
One of my fellows had the speed of him,
Who, almost dead for breath, had scarcely more
Than would make up his message.

LADY MACBETH

Give him tending;
He brings great news.

Exit Messenger

The raven himself is hoarse
That croaks the fatal entrance of Duncan
Under my battlements. Come, you spirits
That tend on mortal thoughts, unsex me here,
And fill me from the crown to the toe top-full
Of direst cruelty! make thick my blood;
Stop up the access and passage to remorse,
That no compunctious visitings of nature
Shake my fell purpose, nor keep peace between
The effect and it! Come to my woman's breasts,
And take my milk for gall, you murdering ministers,
Wherever in your sightless substances

You wait on nature's mischief! Come, thick night,
And pall thee in the dunnest smoke of hell,
That my keen knife see not the wound it makes,
Nor heaven peep through the blanket of the dark,
To cry 'Hold, hold!'

Enter Macbeth

Great Glamis! worthy Cawdor!
Greater than both, by the all-hail hereafter!
Thy letters have transported me beyond
This ignorant present, and I feel now
The future in the instant.

MACBETH

My dearest love,
Duncan comes here to-night.

LADY MACBETH

And when goes hence?

MACBETH

To-morrow, as he purposes.

LADY MACBETH

O, never
Shall sun that morrow see!
Your face, my thane, is as a book where men
May read strange matters. To beguile the time,
Look like the time; bear welcome in your eye,
Your hand, your tongue: look like the innocent flower,
But be the serpent under't. He that's coming
Must be provided for: and you shall put
This night's great business into my dispatch;
Which shall to all our nights and days to come

Give solely sovereign sway and masterdom.

MACBETH

We will speak further.

LADY MACBETH

Only look up clear;
To alter favour ever is to fear:
Leave all the rest to me.

Exeunt

Scene VI. Before Macbeth's castle.

Hautboys and torches. Enter Duncan, Malcolm, Donalbain, Banquo, Lennox, Macduff, Ross, Angus, and Attendants

DUNCAN

This castle hath a pleasant seat; the air
Nimbly and sweetly recommends itself
Unto our gentle senses.

BANQUO

This guest of summer,
The temple-haunting martlet, does approve,
By his loved mansionry, that the heaven's breath
Smells wooingly here: no jutty, frieze,
Buttress, nor coign of vantage, but this bird
Hath made his pendent bed and procreant cradle:
Where they most breed and haunt, I have observed,
The air is delicate.

Enter Lady Macbeth

DUNCAN

See, see, our honour'd hostess!

The love that follows us sometime is our trouble,
Which still we thank as love. Herein I teach you
How you shall bid God 'ild us for your pains,
And thank us for your trouble.

LADY MACBETH

All our service
In every point twice done and then done double
Were poor and single business to contend
Against those honours deep and broad wherewith
Your majesty loads our house: for those of old,
And the late dignities heap'd up to them,
We rest your hermits.

DUNCAN

Where's the thane of Cawdor?
We coursed him at the heels, and had a purpose
To be his purveyor: but he rides well;
And his great love, sharp as his spur, hath holp him
To his home before us. Fair and noble hostess,
We are your guest to-night.

LADY MACBETH

Your servants ever
Have theirs, themselves and what is theirs, in compt,
To make their audit at your highness' pleasure,
Still to return your own.

DUNCAN

Give me your hand;
Conduct me to mine host: we love him highly,
And shall continue our graces towards him.
By your leave, hostess. *Exeunt*

Scene VII. Macbeth's castle.

Hautboys and torches. Enter a Sewer, and divers Servants with dishes and service, and pass over the stage. Then enter Macbeth

MACBETH

If it were done when 'tis done, then 'twere well
It were done quickly: if the assassination
Could trammel up the consequence, and catch
With his surcease success; that but this blow
Might be the be-all and the end-all here,
But here, upon this bank and shoal of time,
We'ld jump the life to come. But in these cases
We still have judgment here; that we but teach
Bloody instructions, which, being taught, return
To plague the inventor: this even-handed justice
Commends the ingredients of our poison'd chalice
To our own lips. He's here in double trust;
First, as I am his kinsman and his subject,
Strong both against the deed; then, as his host,
Who should against his murderer shut the door,
Not bear the knife myself. Besides, this Duncan
Hath borne his faculties so meek, hath been
So clear in his great office, that his virtues
Will plead like angels, trumpet-tongued, against
The deep damnation of his taking-off;
And pity, like a naked new-born babe,
Striding the blast, or heaven's cherubim, horsed
Upon the sightless couriers of the air,
Shall blow the horrid deed in every eye,

That tears shall drown the wind. I have no spur
To prick the sides of my intent, but only
Vaulting ambition, which o'erleaps itself
And falls on the other.

Enter Lady Macbeth

How now! what news?

LADY MACBETH

He has almost supp'd: why have you left the chamber?

MACBETH

Hath he ask'd for me?

LADY MACBETH

Know you not he has?

MACBETH

We will proceed no further in this business:
He hath honour'd me of late; and I have bought
Golden opinions from all sorts of people,
Which would be worn now in their newest gloss,
Not cast aside so soon.

LADY MACBETH

Was the hope drunk
Wherein you dress'd yourself? hath it slept since?
And wakes it now, to look so green and pale
At what it did so freely? From this time
Such I account thy love. Art thou afeard
To be the same in thine own act and valour
As thou art in desire? Wouldst thou have that
Which thou esteem'st the ornament of life,
And live a coward in thine own esteem,
Letting 'I dare not' wait upon 'I would,'

Like the poor cat i'the adage?

MACBETH

Prithee, peace:
I dare do all that may become a man;
Who dares do more is none.

LADY MACBETH

What beast was't, then,
That made you break this enterprise to me?
When you durst do it, then you were a man;
And, to be more than what you were, you would
Be so much more the man. Nor time nor place
Did then adhere, and yet you would make both:
They have made themselves, and that their fitness now
Does unmake you. I have given suck, and know
How tender 'tis to love the babe that milks me:
I would, while it was smiling in my face,
Have pluck'd my nipple from his boneless gums,
And dash'd the brains out, had I so sworn as you
Have done to this.

MACBETH

If we should fail?

LADY MACBETH

We fail!
But screw your courage to the sticking-place,
And we'll not fail. When Duncan is asleep—
Whereto the rather shall his day's hard journey
Soundly invite him—his two chamberlains
Will I with wine and wassail so convince
That memory, the warder of the brain,

Shall be a fume, and the receipt of reason
A limbeck only: when in swinish sleep
Their drenched natures lie as in a death,
What cannot you and I perform upon
The unguarded Duncan? what not put upon
His spongy officers, who shall bear the guilt
Of our great quell?

MACBETH

Bring forth men-children only;
For thy undaunted mettle should compose
Nothing but males. Will it not be received,
When we have mark'd with blood those sleepy two
Of his own chamber and used their very daggers,
That they have done't?

LADY MACBETH

Who dares receive it other,
As we shall make our griefs and clamour roar
Upon his death?

MACBETH

I am settled, and bend up
Each corporal agent to this terrible feat.
Away, and mock the time with fairest show:
False face must hide what the false heart doth know.

Exeunt

***

ACT II

Scene I. Court of Macbeth's castle.

Enter Banquo, and Fleance bearing a torch before him

BANQUO

How goes the night, boy?

FLEANCE

The moon is down; I have not heard the clock.

BANQUO

And she goes down at twelve.

FLEANCE

I take't, 'tis later, sir.

BANQUO

Hold, take my sword. There's husbandry in heaven;
Their candles are all out. Take thee that too.
A heavy summons lies like lead upon me,
And yet I would not sleep: merciful powers,
Restrain in me the cursed thoughts that nature
Gives way to in repose!

Enter Macbeth, and a Servant with a torch

Give me my sword.
Who's there?

MACBETH

A friend.

BANQUO

What, sir, not yet at rest? The king's a-bed:
He hath been in unusual pleasure, and
Sent forth great largess to your offices.
This diamond he greets your wife withal,

By the name of most kind hostess; and shut up
In measureless content.

MACBETH

Being unprepared,
Our will became the servant to defect;
Which else should free have wrought.

BANQUO

All's well.
I dreamt last night of the three weird sisters:
To you they have show'd some truth.

MACBETH

I think not of them:
Yet, when we can entreat an hour to serve,
We would spend it in some words upon that business,
If you would grant the time.

BANQUO

At your kind'st leisure.

MACBETH

If you shall cleave to my consent, when 'tis,
It shall make honour for you.

BANQUO

So I lose none
In seeking to augment it, but still keep
My bosom franchised and allegiance clear,
I shall be counsell'd.

MACBETH

Good repose the while!

BANQUO

Thanks, sir: the like to you!

Exeunt Banquo and Fleance

MACBETH

Go bid thy mistress, when my drink is ready,
She strike upon the bell. Get thee to bed.

Exit Servant

Is this a dagger which I see before me,
The handle toward my hand? Come, let me clutch thee.
I have thee not, and yet I see thee still.
Art thou not, fatal vision, sensible
To feeling as to sight? or art thou but
A dagger of the mind, a false creation,
Proceeding from the heat-oppressed brain?
I see thee yet, in form as palpable
As this which now I draw.
Thou marshall'st me the way that I was going;
And such an instrument I was to use.
Mine eyes are made the fools o'the other senses,
Or else worth all the rest; I see thee still,
And on thy blade and dudgeon gouts of blood,
Which was not so before. There's no such thing:
It is the bloody business which informs
Thus to mine eyes. Now o'er the one halfworld
Nature seems dead, and wicked dreams abuse
The curtain'd sleep; witchcraft celebrates
Pale Hecate's offerings, and wither'd murder,
Alarum'd by his sentinel, the wolf,
Whose howl's his watch, thus with his stealthy pace.
With Tarquin's ravishing strides, towards his design
Moves like a ghost. Thou sure and firm-set earth,

Hear not my steps, which way they walk, for fear
Thy very stones prate of my whereabout,
And take the present horror from the time,
Which now suits with it. Whiles I threat, he lives:
Words to the heat of deeds too cold breath gives.

A bell rings

I go, and it is done; the bell invites me.
Hear it not, Duncan; for it is a knell
That summons thee to heaven or to hell.

Exit

Scene II. The same.

Enter Lady Macbeth

LADY MACBETH

That which hath made them drunk hath made me bold;
What hath quench'd them hath given me fire.
Hark! Peace!
It was the owl that shriek'd, the fatal bellman,
Which gives the stern'st good-night. He is about it:
The doors are open; and the surfeited grooms
Do mock their charge with snores: I have drugg'd
their possets,
That death and nature do contend about them,
Whether they live or die.

MACBETH

[*Within*] Who's there? what, ho!

LADY MACBETH

Alack, I am afraid they have awaked,
And 'tis not done. The attempt and not the deed

Confounds us. Hark! I laid their daggers ready;
He could not miss 'em. Had he not resembled
My father as he slept, I had done't.

Enter Macbeth

My husband!

MACBETH

I have done the deed. Didst thou not hear a noise?

LADY MACBETH

I heard the owl scream and the crickets cry.
Did not you speak?

MACBETH

When?

LADY MACBETH

Now.

MACBETH

As I descended?

LADY MACBETH

Ay.

MACBETH

Hark!
Who lies i'the second chamber?

LADY MACBETH

Donalbain.

MACBETH

This is a sorry sight.

Looking on his hands

LADY MACBETH

A foolish thought, to say a sorry sight.

MACBETH

There's one did laugh in's sleep, and one cried 'Murder!'
That they did wake each other: I stood and heard them:
But they did say their prayers, and address'd them
Again to sleep.

LADY MACBETH

There are two lodged together.

MACBETH

One cried 'God bless us!' and 'Amen' the other;
As they had seen me with these hangman's hands.
Listening their fear, I could not say 'Amen,'
When they did say 'God bless us!'

LADY MACBETH

Consider it not so deeply.

MACBETH

But wherefore could not I pronounce 'Amen'?
I had most need of blessing, and 'Amen'
Stuck in my throat.

LADY MACBETH

These deeds must not be thought
After these ways; so, it will make us mad.

MACBETH

Methought I heard a voice cry 'sleep no more!
Macbeth does murder sleep', the innocent sleep,
Sleep that knits up the ravell'd sleeve of care,
The death of each day's life, sore labour's bath,
Balm of hurt minds, great nature's second course,
Chief nourisher in life's feast'

LADY MACBETH

What do you mean?

MACBETH

Still it cried 'sleep no more!' to all the house:
'Glamis hath murder'd sleep, and therefore Cawdor
Shall sleep no more; Macbeth shall sleep no more.'

LADY MACBETH

Who was it that thus cried? Why, worthy thane,
You do unbend your noble strength, to think
So brainsickly of things. Go get some water,
And wash this filthy witness from your hand.
Why did you bring these daggers from the place?
They must lie there: go carry them; and smear
The sleepy grooms with blood.

MACBETH

I'll go no more:
I am afraid to think what I have done;
Look on't again I dare not.

LADY MACBETH

Infirm of purpose!
Give me the daggers: the sleeping and the dead
Are but as pictures: 'tis the eye of childhood
That fears a painted devil. If he do bleed,
I'll gild the faces of the grooms withal;
For it must seem their guilt.

Exit. Knocking within

MACBETH

Whence is that knocking?
How is't with me, when every noise appals me?

What hands are here? ha! they pluck out mine eyes.
Will all great Neptune's ocean wash this blood
Clean from my hand? No, this my hand will rather
The multitudinous seas in incarnadine,
Making the green one red.

Re-enter Lady Macbeth

LADY MACBETH

My hands are of your colour; but I shame
To wear a heart so white.

Knocking within

I hear a knocking
At the south entry: retire we to our chamber;
A little water clears us of this deed:
How easy is it, then! Your constancy
Hath left you unattended.

Knocking within

Hark! more knocking.
Get on your nightgown, lest occasion call us,
And show us to be watchers. Be not lost
So poorly in your thoughts.

MACBETH

To know my deed, 'twere best not know myself.

Knocking within

Wake Duncan with thy knocking! I would thou couldst!

Exeunt

Scene III. The same.

Knocking within. Enter a Porter

PORTER

Here's a knocking indeed! If a man were porter of hell-gate, he should have old turning the key.

Knocking within

Knock, knock, knock! Who's there, i'the name of Beelzebub? Here's a farmer, that hanged himself on the expectation of plenty: come in time; have napkins enow about you; here you'll sweat for't.

Knocking within

Knock, knock! Who's there, in the other devil's name? Faith, here's an equivocator, that could swear in both the scales against either scale; who committed treason enough for God's sake, yet could not equivocate to heaven: O, come in, equivocator.

Knocking within

Knock, knock, knock! Who's there? Faith, here's an English tailor come hither, for stealing out of a French hose: come in, tailor; here you may roast your goose.

Knocking within

Knock,
knock; never at quiet! What are you? But
this place is too cold for hell. I'll devil-porter
it no further: I had thought to have let in
some of all professions that go the primrose
way to the everlasting bonfire.

Knocking within

Anon, anon! I pray you, remember the porter.

Opens the gate.

Enter Macduff and Lennox

MACDUFF

Was it so late, friend, ere you went to bed,
That you do lie so late?

PORTER

'Faith sir, we were carousing till the
second cock: and drink, sir, is a great
provoker of three things.

MACDUFF

What three things does drink especially provoke?

PORTER

Marry, sir, nose-painting, sleep, and
urine. Lechery, sir, it provokes, and unprovokes;
it provokes the desire, but it takes
away the performance: therefore, much drink
may be said to be an equivocator with lechery:
it makes him, and it mars him; it sets
him on, and it takes him off; it persuades him,
and disheartens him; makes him stand to, and

not stand to; in conclusion, equivocates him in a sleep, and, giving him the lie, leaves him.

MACDUFF

I believe drink gave thee the lie last night.

PORTER

That it did, sir, i'the very throat on me: but I requited him for his lie; and, I think, being too strong for him, though he took up my legs sometime, yet I made a shift to cast him.

MACDUFF

Is thy master stirring?

Enter Macbeth

Our knocking has awaked him; here he comes.

LENNOX

Good morrow, noble sir.

MACBETH

Good morrow, both.

MACDUFF

Is the king stirring, worthy thane?

MACBETH

Not yet.

MACDUFF

He did command me to call timely on him:
I have almost slipp'd the hour.

MACBETH

I'll bring you to him.

MACDUFF

I know this is a joyful trouble to you;

But yet 'tis one.

MACBETH

The labour we delight in physics pain.
This is the door.

MACDUFF

I'll make so bold to call,
For 'tis my limited service.

Exit

LENNOX

Goes the king hence to-day?

MACBETH

He does: he did appoint so.

LENNOX

The night has been unruly: where we lay,
Our chimneys were blown down; and, as they say,
Lamentings heard i'the air; strange screams of death,
And prophesying with accents terrible
Of dire combustion and confused events
New hatch'd to the woeful time: the obscure bird
Clamour'd the livelong night: some say, the earth
Was feverous and did shake.

MACBETH

'Twas a rough night.

LENNOX

My young remembrance cannot parallel
A fellow to it.

Re-enter Macduff

MACDUFF

O horror, horror, horror! Tongue nor heart

Cannot conceive nor name thee!

MACBETH, LENNOX

What's the matter.

MACDUFF

Confusion now hath made his masterpiece!
Most sacrilegious murder hath broke ope
The Lord's anointed temple, and stole thence
The life o'the building!

MACBETH

What is't you say? the life?

LENNOX

Mean you his majesty?

MACDUFF

Approach the chamber, and destroy your sight
With a new Gorgon: do not bid me speak;
See, and then speak yourselves.

Exeunt Macbeth and Lennox

Awake, awake!
Ring the alarum-bell. Murder and treason!
Banquo and Donalbain! Malcolm! awake!
Shake off this downy sleep, death's counterfeit,
And look on death itself! up, up, and see
The great doom's image! Malcolm! Banquo!
As from your graves rise up, and walk like sprites,
To countenance this horror! Ring the bell.

Bell rings

Enter Lady Macbeth

LADY MACBETH

What's the business,

That such a hideous trumpet calls to parley
The sleepers of the house? speak, speak!

MACDUFF

O gentle lady,
'Tis not for you to hear what I can speak:
The repetition, in a woman's ear,
Would murder as it fell.

Enter Banquo

O Banquo, Banquo,
Our royal master's murder'd!

LADY MACBETH

Woe, alas!
What, in our house?

BANQUO

Too cruel any where.
Dear Duff, I prithee, contradict thyself,
And say it is not so.

Re-enter Macbeth and Lennox, with Ross

MACBETH

Had I but died an hour before this chance,
I had lived a blessed time; for, from this instant,
There's nothing serious in mortality:
All is but toys: renown and grace is dead;
The wine of life is drawn, and the mere lees
Is left this vault to brag of.

Enter Malcolm and Donalbain

DONALBAIN

What is amiss?

MACBETH

You are, and do not know't:
The spring, the head, the fountain of your blood
Is stopp'd; the very source of it is stopp'd.

MACDUFF

Your royal father's murder'd.

MALCOLM

O, by whom?

LENNOX

Those of his chamber, as it seem'd, had done 't:
Their hands and faces were an badged with blood;
So were their daggers, which unwiped we found
Upon their pillows:
They stared, and were distracted; no man's life
Was to be trusted with them.

MACBETH

O, yet I do repent me of my fury,
That I did kill them.

MACDUFF

Wherefore did you so?

MACBETH

Who can be wise, amazed, temperate and furious,
Loyal and neutral, in a moment? No man:
The expedition my violent love
Outrun the pauser, reason. Here lay Duncan,
His silver skin laced with his golden blood;
And his gash'd stabs look'd like a breach in nature
For ruin's wasteful entrance: there, the murderers,
Steep'd in the colours of their trade, their daggers

Unmannerly breech'd with gore: who could refrain,
That had a heart to love, and in that heart
Courage to make's love known?

LADY MACBETH

Help me hence, ho!

MACDUFF

Look to the lady.

MALCOLM

[*Aside to Donalbain*] Why do we hold our tongues,
That most may claim this argument for ours?

DONALBAIN

[*Aside to Malcolm*] What should be spoken here, where our fate,
Hid in an auger-hole, may rush, and seize us?
Let's away;
Our tears are not yet brew'd.

MALCOLM

[*Aside to Donalbain*] Nor our strong sorrow
Upon the foot of motion.

BANQUO

Look to the lady:

Lady Macbeth is carried out

And when we have our naked frailties hid,
That suffer in exposure, let us meet,
And question this most bloody piece of work,
To know it further. Fears and scruples shake us:
In the great hand of God I stand; and thence
Against the undivulged pretence I fight
Of treasonous malice.

MACDUFF

And so do I.

ALL

So all.

MACBETH

Let's briefly put on manly readiness,
And meet i'the hall together.

ALL

Well contented.

Exeunt all but Malcolm and Donalbain.

MALCOLM

What will you do? Let's not consort with them:
To show an unfelt sorrow is an office
Which the false man does easy. I'll to England.

DONALBAIN

To Ireland, I; our separated fortune
Shall keep us both the safer: where we are,
There's daggers in men's smiles: the near in blood,
The nearer bloody.

MALCOLM

This murderous shaft that's shot
Hath not yet lighted, and our safest way
Is to avoid the aim. Therefore, to horse;
And let us not be dainty of leave-taking,
But shift away: there's warrant in that theft
Which steals itself, when there's no mercy left.

Exeunt

Scene IV. Outside Macbeth's castle.

Enter Ross and an old Man

OLD MAN

Threescore and ten I can remember well:
Within the volume of which time I have seen
Hours dreadful and things strange; but this sore night
Hath trifled former knowings.

ROSS

Ah, good father,
Thou seest, the heavens, as troubled with man's act,
Threaten his bloody stage: by the clock, 'tis day,
And yet dark night strangles the travelling lamp:
Is't night's predominance, or the day's shame,
That darkness does the face of earth entomb,
When living light should kiss it?

OLD MAN

'Tis unnatural,
Even like the deed that's done. On Tuesday last,
A falcon, towering in her pride of place,
Was by a mousing owl hawk'd at and kill'd.

ROSS

And Duncan's horses—a thing most strange and certain—
Beauteous and swift, the minions of their race,
Turn'd wild in nature, broke their stalls, flung out,
Contending 'gainst obedience, as they would make
War with mankind.

OLD MAN

'Tis said they eat each other.

ROSS

They did so, to the amazement of mine eyes
That look'd upon't. Here comes the good Macduff.

Enter Macduff

How goes the world, sir, now?

MACDUFF

Why, see you not?

ROSS

Is't known who did this more than bloody deed?

MACDUFF

Those that Macbeth hath slain.

ROSS

Alas, the day!
What good could they pretend?

MACDUFF

They were suborn'd:
Malcolm and Donalbain, the king's two sons,
Are stol'n away and fled; which puts upon them
Suspicion of the deed.

ROSS

'Gainst nature still!
Thriftless ambition, that wilt ravin up
Thine own life's means! Then 'tis most like
The sovereignty will fall upon Macbeth.

MACDUFF

He is already named, and gone to Scone
To be invested.

ROSS

Where is Duncan's body?

MACDUFF

Carried to Colmekill,
The sacred storehouse of his predecessors,
And guardian of their bones.

ROSS

Will you to Scone?

MACDUFF

No, cousin, I'll to Fife.

ROSS

Well, I will thither.

MACDUFF

Well, may you see things well done there: Adieu!
Lest our old robes sit easier than our new!

ROSS

Farewell, father.

OLD MAN

God's benison go with you; and with those
That would make good of bad, and friends of foes!

Exeunt

***

ACT III

Scene I. Forres. The palace.

Enter Banquo

BANQUO

Thou hast it now: king, Cawdor, Glamis, all,
As the weird women promised, and, I fear,

Thou play'dst most foully for't: yet it was said
It should not stand in thy posterity,
But that myself should be the root and father
Of many kings. If there come truth from them—
As upon thee, Macbeth, their speeches shine—
Why, by the verities on thee made good,
May they not be my oracles as well,
And set me up in hope? But hush! no more.

Sennet sounded. Enter Macbeth, as king, Lady Macbeth, as queen, Lennox, Ross, Lords, Ladies, and Attendants

MACBETH

Here's our chief guest.

LADY MACBETH

If he had been forgotten,
It had been as a gap in our great feast,
And all-thing unbecoming.

MACBETH

To-night we hold a solemn supper sir,
And I'll request your presence.

BANQUO

Let your highness
Command upon me; to the which my duties
Are with a most indissoluble tie
For ever knit.

MACBETH

Ride you this afternoon?

BANQUO

Ay, my good lord.

MACBETH

We should have else desired your good advice,
Which still hath been both grave and prosperous,
In this day's council; but we'll take to-morrow.
Is't far you ride?

Banquo

As far, my lord, as will fill up the time
'Twixt this and supper: go not my horse the better,
I must become a borrower of the night
For a dark hour or twain.

MACBETH

Fail not our feast.

BANQUO

My lord, I will not.

MACBETH

We hear, our bloody cousins are bestow'd
In England and in Ireland, not confessing
Their cruel parricide, filling their hearers
With strange invention: but of that to-morrow,
When therewithal we shall have cause of state
Craving us jointly. Hie you to horse: Adieu,
Till you return at night. Goes Fleance with you?

BANQUO

Ay, my good lord: our time does call upon's.

MACBETH

I wish your horses swift and sure of foot;
And so I do commend you to their backs. Farewell.

Exit Banquo

Let every man be master of his time

Till seven at night: to make society
The sweeter welcome, we will keep ourself
Till supper-time alone: while then, God be with you!

Exeunt all but Macbeth, and an attendant

Sirrah, a word with you: attend those men
Our pleasure?

ATTENDANT

They are, my lord, without the palace gate.

MACBETH

Bring them before us.

Exit Attendant

To be thus is nothing;
But to be safely thus.—Our fears in Banquo
Stick deep; and in his royalty of nature
Reigns that which would be fear'd: 'tis much he dares;
And, to that dauntless temper of his mind,
He hath a wisdom that doth guide his valour
To act in safety. There is none but he
Whose being I do fear: and, under him,
My Genius is rebuked; as, it is said,
Mark Antony's was by Caesar. He chid the sisters
When first they put the name of king upon me,
And bade them speak to him: then prophet-like
They hail'd him father to a line of kings:
Upon my head they placed a fruitless crown,
And put a barren sceptre in my gripe,
Thence to be wrench'd with an unlineal hand,
No son of mine succeeding. If 't be so,
For Banquo's issue have I filed my mind;

For them the gracious Duncan have I murder'd;
Put rancours in the vessel of my peace
Only for them; and mine eternal jewel
Given to the common enemy of man,
To make them kings, the seed of Banquo kings!
Rather than so, come fate into the list.
And champion me to the utterance! Who's there!

Re-enter Attendant, with two Murderers

Now go to the door, and stay there till we call.

Exit Attendant

Was it not yesterday we spoke together?

FIRST MURDERER

It was, so please your highness.

MACBETH

Well then, now
Have you consider'd of my speeches? Know
That it was he in the times past which held you
So under fortune, which you thought had been
Our innocent self: This I made good to you
In our last conference, pass'd in probation with you,
How you were borne in hand, how cross'd, the instruments,
Who wrought with them, and all things else that might
To half a soul and to a notion crazed
Say 'Thus did Banquo.'

FIRST MURDERER

You made it known to us.

MACBETH

I did so, and went further, which is now
Our point of second meeting. Do you find

Your patience so predominant in your nature
That you can let this go? Are you so gospell'd
To pray for this good man and for his issue,
Whose heavy hand hath bow'd you to the grave
And beggar'd yours for ever?

FIRST MURDERER

We are men, my liege.

MACBETH

Ay, in the catalogue ye go for men;
As hounds and greyhounds, mongrels, spaniels, curs,
Shoughs, water-rugs and demi-wolves, are clept
All by the name of dogs: the valued file
Distinguishes the swift, the slow, the subtle,
The housekeeper, the hunter, every one
According to the gift which bounteous nature
Hath in him closed; whereby he does receive
Particular addition. from the bill
That writes them all alike: and so of men.
Now, if you have a station in the file,
Not i'the worst rank of manhood, say't;
And I will put that business in your bosoms,
Whose execution takes your enemy off,
Grapples you to the heart and love of us,
Who wear our health but sickly in his life,
Which in his death were perfect.

SECOND MURDERER

I am one, my liege,
Whom the vile blows and buffets of the world
Have so incensed that I am reckless what

I do to spite the world.

FIRST MURDERER

And I another
So weary with disasters, tugg'd with fortune,
That I would set my lie on any chance,
To mend it, or be rid on't.

MACBETH

Both of you
Know Banquo was your enemy.

BOTH MURDERERS

True, my lord.

MACBETH

So is he mine; and in such bloody distance,
That every minute of his being thrusts
Against my near'st of life: and though I could
With barefaced power sweep him from my sight
And bid my will avouch it, yet I must not,
For certain friends that are both his and mine,
Whose loves I may not drop, but wail his fall
Who I myself struck down; and thence it is,
That I to your assistance do make love,
Masking the business from the common eye
For sundry weighty reasons.

SECOND MURDERER

We shall, my lord,
Perform what you command us.

FIRST MURDERER

Though our lives—

MACBETH

Your spirits shine through you. Within this hour at most
I will advise you where to plant yourselves;
Acquaint you with the perfect spy o'the time,
The moment on't; for't must be done to-night,
And something from the palace; always thought
That I require a clearness: and with him—
To leave no rubs nor botches in the work—
Fleance his son, that keeps him company,
Whose absence is no less material to me
Than is his father's, must embrace the fate
Of that dark hour. Resolve yourselves apart:
I'll come to you anon.

BOTH MURDERERS

We are resolved, my lord.

MACBETH

I'll call upon you straight: abide within.

Exeunt Murderers

It is concluded. Banquo, thy soul's flight,
If it find heaven, must find it out to-night.

Exit

Scene II. The palace.

Enter Lady Macbeth and a Servant

LADY MACBETH

Is Banquo gone from court?

SERVANT

Ay, madam, but returns again to-night.

LADY MACBETH

Say to the king, I would attend his leisure
For a few words.

SERVANT

Madam, I will.

Exit

LADY MACBETH

Nought's had, all's spent,
Where our desire is got without content:
'Tis safer to be that which we destroy
Than by destruction dwell in doubtful joy.

Enter Macbeth

How now, my lord! why do you keep alone,
Of sorriest fancies your companions making,
Using those thoughts which should indeed have died
With them they think on? Things without all remedy
Should be without regard: what's done is done.

MACBETH

We have scotch'd the snake, not kill'd it:
She'll close and be herself, whilst our poor malice
Remains in danger of her former tooth.
But let the frame of things disjoint, both the worlds suffer,
Ere we will eat our meal in fear and sleep
In the affliction of these terrible dreams
That shake us nightly: better be with the dead,
Whom we, to gain our peace, have sent to peace,
Than on the torture of the mind to lie
In restless ecstasy. Duncan is in his grave;
After life's fitful fever he sleeps well;

Treason has done his worst: nor steel, nor poison,
Malice domestic, foreign levy, nothing,
Can touch him further.

LADY MACBETH

Come on;
Gentle my lord, sleek o'er your rugged looks;
Be bright and jovial among your guests to-night.

MACBETH

So shall I, love; and so, I pray, be you:
Let your remembrance apply to Banquo;
Present him eminence, both with eye and tongue:
Unsafe the while, that we
Must lave our honours in these flattering streams,
And make our faces vizards to our hearts,
Disguising what they are.

LADY MACBETH

You must leave this.

MACBETH

O, full of scorpions is my mind, dear wife!
Thou know'st that Banquo, and his Fleance, lives.

LADY MACBETH

But in them nature's copy's not eterne.

MACBETH

There's comfort yet; they are assailable;
Then be thou jocund: ere the bat hath flown
His cloister'd flight, ere to black Hecate's summons
The shard-borne beetle with his drowsy hums
Hath rung night's yawning peal, there shall be done
A deed of dreadful note.

LADY MACBETH

What's to be done?

MACBETH

Be innocent of the knowledge, dearest chuck,
Till thou applaud the deed. Come, seeling night,
Scarf up the tender eye of pitiful day;
And with thy bloody and invisible hand
Cancel and tear to pieces that great bond
Which keeps me pale! Light thickens; and the crow
Makes wing to the rooky wood:
Good things of day begin to droop and drowse;
While night's black agents to their preys do rouse.
Thou marvell'st at my words: but hold thee still;
Things bad begun make strong themselves by ill.
So, prithee, go with me.

Exeunt

Scene III. A park near the palace.

Enter three Murderers

FIRST MURDERER

But who did bid thee join with us?

THIRD MURDERER

Macbeth.

SECOND MURDERER

He needs not our mistrust, since he delivers
Our offices and what we have to do
To the direction just.

FIRST MURDERER

Then stand with us.

The west yet glimmers with some streaks of day:
Now spurs the lated traveller apace
To gain the timely inn; and near approaches
The subject of our watch.

THIRD MURDERER

Hark! I hear horses.

BANQUO

[*Within*] Give us a light there, ho!

SECOND MURDERER

Then 'tis he: the rest
That are within the note of expectation
Already are i'the court.

FIRST MURDERER

His horses go about.

THIRD MURDERER

Almost a mile: but he does usually,
So all men do, from hence to the palace gate
Make it their walk.

SECOND MURDERER

A light, a light!

Enter Banquo, and Fleance with a torch

THIRD MURDERER

'Tis he.

FIRST MURDERER

Stand to't.

BANQUO

It will be rain to-night.

FIRST MURDERER

Let it come down.

They set upon Banquo

BANQUO

O, treachery! Fly, good Fleance, fly, fly, fly!
Thou mayst revenge. O slave!

Dies. Fleance escapes

THIRD MURDERER

Who did strike out the light?

FIRST MURDERER

Wast not the way?

THIRD MURDERER

There's but one down; the son is fled.

SECOND MURDERER

We have lost
Best half of our affair.

FIRST MURDERER

Well, let's away, and say how much is done.

Exeunt

Scene IV. The same. Hall in the palace.

A banquet prepared. Enter Macbeth, Lady Macbeth, Ross, Lennox, Lords, and Attendants

MACBETH

You know your own degrees; sit down: At first
And last the hearty welcome.

LORDS

Thanks to your majesty.

MACBETH

Ourself will mingle with society,
And play the humble host.

Our hostess keeps her state, but in best time
We will require her welcome.

LADY MACBETH

Pronounce it for me, sir, to all our friends;
For my heart speaks they are welcome.

First Murderer appears at the door

MACBETH

See, they encounter thee with their hearts' thanks.
Both sides are even: here I'll sit i'the midst:
Be large in mirth; anon we'll drink a measure
The table round.

Approaching the door

There's blood on thy face.

FIRST MURDERER

'Tis Banquo's then.

MACBETH

'Tis better thee without than he within.
Is he dispatch'd?

FIRST MURDERER

My lord, his throat is cut; that I did for him.

MACBETH

Thou art the best o'the cut-throats: yet he's good
That did the like for Fleance: if thou didst it,
Thou art the nonpareil.

FIRST MURDERER

Most royal sir,
Fleance is 'scaped.

MACBETH

Then comes my fit again: I had else been perfect,

Whole as the marble, founded as the rock,
As broad and general as the casing air:
But now I am cabin'd, cribb'd, confined, bound in
To saucy doubts and fears. But Banquo's safe?

FIRST MURDERER

Ay, my good lord: safe in a ditch he bides,
With twenty trenched gashes on his head;
The least a death to nature.

MACBETH

Thanks for that:
There the grown serpent lies; the worm that's fled
Hath nature that in time will venom breed,
No teeth for the present. Get thee gone: to-morrow
We'll hear, ourselves, again.

Exit Murderer

LADY MACBETH

My royal lord,
You do not give the cheer: the feast is sold
That is not often vouch'd, while 'tis a-making,
'Tis given with welcome: to feed were best at home;
From thence the sauce to meat is ceremony;
Meeting were bare without it.

MACBETH

Sweet remembrancer!
Now, good digestion wait on appetite,
And health on both!

LENNOX

May't please your highness sit.

The Ghost Of Banquo enters, and sits in Macbeth's place

MACBETH

Here had we now our country's honour roof'd,
Were the graced person of our Banquo present;
Who may I rather challenge for unkindness
Than pity for mischance!

ROSS

His absence, sir,
Lays blame upon his promise. Please't your highness
To grace us with your royal company.

MACBETH

The table's full.

LENNOX

Here is a place reserved, sir.

MACBETH

Where?

LENNOX

Here, my good lord. What is't that moves your highness?

MACBETH

Which of you have done this?

LORDS

What, my good lord?

MACBETH

Thou canst not say I did it: never shake
Thy gory locks at me.

ROSS

Gentlemen, rise: his highness is not well.

LADY MACBETH

Sit, worthy friends: my lord is often thus,
And hath been from his youth: pray you, keep seat;

The fit is momentary; upon a thought
He will again be well: if much you note him,
You shall offend him and extend his passion:
Feed, and regard him not. Are you a man?

MACBETH

Ay, and a bold one, that dare look on that
Which might appal the devil.

LADY MACBETH

O proper stuff!
This is the very painting of your fear:
This is the air-drawn dagger which, you said,
Led you to Duncan. O, these flaws and starts,
Impostors to true fear, would well become
A woman's story at a winter's fire,
Authorized by her grandam. Shame itself!
Why do you make such faces? When all's done,
You look but on a stool.

MACBETH

Prithee, see there! behold! look! lo! how say you?
Why, what care I? If thou canst nod, speak too.
If charnel-houses and our graves must send
Those that we bury back, our monuments
Shall be the maws of kites.

Ghost of Banquo vanishes

LADY MACBETH

What, quite unmann'd in folly?

MACBETH

If I stand here, I saw him.

LADY MACBETH

Fie, for shame!

MACBETH

Blood hath been shed ere now, i'the olden time,
Ere human statute purged the gentle weal;
Ay, and since too, murders have been perform'd
Too terrible for the ear: the times have been,
That, when the brains were out, the man would die,
And there an end; but now they rise again,
With twenty mortal murders on their crowns,
And push us from our stools: this is more strange
Than such a murder is.

LADY MACBETH

My worthy lord,
Your noble friends do lack you.

MACBETH

I do forget.
Do not muse at me, my most worthy friends,
I have a strange infirmity, which is nothing
To those that know me. Come, love and health to all;
Then I'll sit down. Give me some wine; fill full.
I drink to the general joy o'the whole table,
And to our dear friend Banquo, whom we miss;
Would he were here! to all, and him, we thirst,
And all to all.

LORDS

Our duties, and the pledge.

Re-enter Ghost of Banquo

MACBETH

Avaunt! and quit my sight! let the earth hide thee!
Thy bones are marrowless, thy blood is cold;
Thou hast no speculation in those eyes
Which thou dost glare with!

LADY MACBETH

Think of this, good peers,
But as a thing of custom: 'tis no other;
Only it spoils the pleasure of the time.

MACBETH

What man dare, I dare:
Approach thou like the rugged Russian bear,
The arm'd rhinoceros, or the Hyrcan tiger;
Take any shape but that, and my firm nerves
Shall never tremble: or be alive again,
And dare me to the desert with thy sword;
If trembling I inhabit then, protest me
The baby of a girl. Hence, horrible shadow!
Unreal mockery, hence!

Ghost of Banquo vanishes

Why, so: being gone,
I am a man again. Pray you, sit still.

LADY MACBETH

You have displaced the mirth, broke the good meeting,
With most admired disorder.

MACBETH

Can such things be,
And overcome us like a summer's cloud,
Without our special wonder? You make me strange

Even to the disposition that I owe,
When now I think you can behold such sights,
And keep the natural ruby of your cheeks,
When mine is blanched with fear.

ROSS

What sights, my lord?

LADY MACBETH

I pray you, speak not; he grows worse and worse;
Question enrages him. At once, good night:
Stand not upon the order of your going,
But go at once.

LENNOX

Good night; and better health
Attend his majesty!

LADY MACBETH

A kind good night to all!

Exeunt all but Macbeth and Lady Macbeth

MACBETH

It will have blood; they say, blood will have blood:
Stones have been known to move and trees to speak;
Augurs and understood relations have
By magot-pies and choughs and rooks brought forth
The secret'st man of blood. What is the night?

LADY MACBETH

Almost at odds with morning, which is which.

MACBETH

How say'st thou, that Macduff denies his person
At our great bidding?

LADY MACBETH

Did you send to him, sir?

MACBETH

I hear it by the way; but I will send:
There's not a one of them but in his house
I keep a servant fee'd. I will to-morrow,
And betimes I will, to the weird sisters:
More shall they speak; for now I am bent to know,
By the worst means, the worst. For mine own good,
All causes shall give way: I am in blood
Stepp'd in so far that, should I wade no more,
Returning were as tedious as go o'er:
Strange things I have in head, that will to hand;
Which must be acted ere they may be scann'd.

LADY MACBETH

You lack the season of all natures, sleep.

MACBETH

Come, we'll to sleep. My strange and self-abuse
Is the initiate fear that wants hard use:
We are yet but young in deed.

Exeunt

Scene V. A Heath.

Thunder. Enter the three Witches meeting Hecate

FIRST WITCH

Why, how now, Hecate! you look angerly.

HECATE

Have I not reason, beldams as you are,
Saucy and overbold? How did you dare

To trade and traffic with Macbeth
In riddles and affairs of death;
And I, the mistress of your charms,
The close contriver of all harms,
Was never call'd to bear my part,
Or show the glory of our art?
And, which is worse, all you have done
Hath been but for a wayward son,
Spiteful and wrathful, who, as others do,
Loves for his own ends, not for you.
But make amends now: get you gone,
And at the pit of Acheron
Meet me i'the morning: thither he
Will come to know his destiny:
Your vessels and your spells provide,
Your charms and every thing beside.
I am for the air; this night I'll spend
Unto a dismal and a fatal end:
Great business must be wrought ere noon:
Upon the corner of the moon
There hangs a vaporous drop profound;
I'll catch it ere it come to ground:
And that distill'd by magic sleights
Shall raise such artificial sprites
As by the strength of their illusion
Shall draw him on to his confusion:
He shall spurn fate, scorn death, and bear
He hopes 'bove wisdom, grace and fear:
And you all know, security

Is mortals' chiefest enemy.

Music and a song within: 'Come away, come away,' etc.

Hark! I am call'd; my little spirit, see,
Sits in a foggy cloud, and stays for me.

Exit

FIRST WITCH

Come, let's make haste; she'll soon be back again.

Exeunt

Scene VI. Forres. The palace.

Enter Lennox and another Lord

LENNOX

My former speeches have but hit your thoughts,
Which can interpret further: only, I say,
Things have been strangely borne. The gracious Duncan
Was pitied of Macbeth: marry, he was dead:
And the right-valiant Banquo walk'd too late;
Whom, you may say, if't please you, Fleance kill'd,
For Fleance fled: men must not walk too late.
Who cannot want the thought how monstrous
It was for Malcolm and for Donalbain
To kill their gracious father? damned fact!
How it did grieve Macbeth! did he not straight
In pious rage the two delinquents tear,
That were the slaves of drink and thralls of sleep?
Was not that nobly done? Ay, and wisely too;
For 'twould have anger'd any heart alive
To hear the men deny't. So that, I say,
He has borne all things well: and I do think

That had he Duncan's sons under his key—
As, an't please heaven, he shall not—they should find
What 'twere to kill a father; so should Fleance.
But, peace! for from broad words and 'cause he fail'd
His presence at the tyrant's feast, I hear
Macduff lives in disgrace: sir, can you tell
Where he bestows himself?

LORD

The son of Duncan,
From whom this tyrant holds the due of birth
Lives in the English court, and is received
Of the most pious Edward with such grace
That the malevolence of fortune nothing
Takes from his high respect: thither Macduff
Is gone to pray the holy king, upon his aid
To wake Northumberland and warlike Siward:
That, by the help of these—with Him above
To ratify the work—we may again
Give to our tables meat, sleep to our nights,
Free from our feasts and banquets bloody knives,
Do faithful homage and receive free honours:
All which we pine for now: and this report
Hath so exasperate the king that he
Prepares for some attempt of war.

LENNOX

Sent he to Macduff?

LORD

He did: and with an absolute 'Sir, not I,'
The cloudy messenger turns me his back,

And hums, as who should say 'You'll rue the time
That clogs me with this answer.'

LENNOX

And that well might
Advise him to a caution, to hold what distance
His wisdom can provide. Some holy angel
Fly to the court of England and unfold
His message ere he come, that a swift blessing
May soon return to this our suffering country
Under a hand accursed!

LORD

I'll send my prayers with him.

Exeunt

***

ACT IV

Scene I. A cavern. In the middle, a boiling cauldron.

Thunder. Enter the three Witches

FIRST WITCH

Thrice the brinded cat hath mew'd.

SECOND WITCH

Thrice and once the hedge-pig whined.

THIRD WITCH

Harpier cries 'Tis time, 'tis time.

FIRST WITCH

Round about the cauldron go;
In the poison'd entrails throw.

Toad, that under cold stone
Days and nights has thirty-one
Swelter'd venom sleeping got,
Boil thou first i'the charmed pot.

ALL

Double, double toil and trouble;
Fire burn, and cauldron bubble.

SECOND WITCH

Fillet of a fenny snake,
In the cauldron boil and bake;
Eye of newt and toe of frog,
Wool of bat and tongue of dog,
Adder's fork and blind-worm's sting,
Lizard's leg and owlet's wing,
For a charm of powerful trouble,
Like a hell-broth boil and bubble.

ALL

Double, double toil and trouble;
Fire burn and cauldron bubble.

THIRD WITCH

Scale of dragon, tooth of wolf,
Witches' mummy, maw and gulf
Of the ravin'd salt-sea shark,
Root of hemlock digg'd i'the dark,
Liver of blaspheming Jew,
Gall of goat, and slips of yew
Silver'd in the moon's eclipse,
Nose of Turk and Tartar's lips,
Finger of birth-strangled babe

Ditch-deliver'd by a drab,
Make the gruel thick and slab:
Add thereto a tiger's chaudron,
For the ingredients of our cauldron.

ALL

Double, double toil and trouble;
Fire burn and cauldron bubble.

SECOND WITCH

Cool it with a baboon's blood,
Then the charm is firm and good.

Enter Hecate to the other three Witches

HECATE

O well done! I commend your pains;
And every one shall share i'the gains;
And now about the cauldron sing,
Live elves and fairies in a ring,
Enchanting all that you put in.

Music and a song: 'Black spirits,' etc

Hecate retires

SECOND WITCH

By the pricking of my thumbs,
Something wicked this way comes.
Open, locks,
Whoever knocks!

Enter Macbeth

MACBETH

How now, you secret, black, and midnight hags!
What is't you do?

ALL

A deed without a name.

MACBETH

I conjure you, by that which you profess,
Howe'er you come to know it, answer me:
Though you untie the winds and let them fight
Against the churches; though the yesty waves
Confound and swallow navigation up;
Though bladed corn be lodged and trees blown down;
Though castles topple on their warders' heads;
Though palaces and pyramids do slope
Their heads to their foundations; though the treasure
Of nature's germens tumble all together,
Even till destruction sicken; answer me
To what I ask you.

FIRST WITCH

Speak.

SECOND WITCH

Demand.

THIRD WITCH

We'll answer.

FIRST WITCH

Say, if thou'dst rather hear it from our mouths,
Or from our masters?

MACBETH

Call 'em; let me see 'em.

FIRST WITCH

Pour in sow's blood, that hath eaten
Her nine farrow; grease that's sweaten

From the murderer's gibbet throw
Into the flame.

ALL

Come, high or low;
Thyself and office deftly show!

Thunder. First Apparition: an armed Head

MACBETH

Tell me, thou unknown power—

FIRST WITCH

He knows thy thought:
Hear his speech, but say thou nought.

FIRST APPARITION

Macbeth! Macbeth! Macbeth! beware Macduff;
Beware the thane of Fife. Dismiss me. Enough.

Descends

MACBETH

Whate'er thou art, for thy good caution, thanks;
Thou hast harp'd my fear aright: but one word more—

FIRST WITCH

He will not be commanded: here's another,
More potent than the first.

Thunder. Second Apparition: A bloody Child

SECOND APPARITION

Macbeth! Macbeth! Macbeth!

MACBETH

Had I three ears, I'ld hear thee.

SECOND APPARITION

Be bloody, bold, and resolute; laugh to scorn
The power of man, for none of woman born

Shall harm Macbeth.

Descends

MACBETH

Then live, Macduff: what need I fear of thee?
But yet I'll make assurance double sure,
And take a bond of fate: thou shalt not live;
That I may tell pale-hearted fear it lies,
And sleep in spite of thunder.

Thunder. Third Apparition: a Child crowned, with a tree in his hand

What is this
That rises like the issue of a king,
And wears upon his baby-brow the round
And top of sovereignty?

ALL

Listen, but speak not to't.

THIRD APPARITION

Be lion-mettled, proud; and take no care
Who chafes, who frets, or where conspirers are:
Macbeth shall never vanquish'd be until
Great Birnam wood to high Dunsinane hill
Shall come against him.

Descends

MACBETH

That will never be
Who can impress the forest, bid the tree
Unfix his earth-bound root? Sweet bodements! good!
Rebellion's head, rise never till the wood
Of Birnam rise, and our high-placed Macbeth

Shall live the lease of nature, pay his breath
To time and mortal custom. Yet my heart
Throbs to know one thing: tell me, if your art
Can tell so much: shall Banquo's issue ever
Reign in this kingdom?

ALL

Seek to know no more.

MACBETH

I will be satisfied: deny me this,
And an eternal curse fall on you! Let me know.
Why sinks that cauldron? and what noise is this?

Hautboys

FIRST WITCH

Show!

SECOND WITCH

Show!

THIRD WITCH

Show!

ALL

Show his eyes, and grieve his heart;
Come like shadows, so depart!

A show of Eight Kings, the last with a glass in his hand; Ghost of Banquo following

MACBETH

Thou art too like the spirit of Banquo: down!
Thy crown does sear mine eye-balls. And thy hair,
Thou other gold-bound brow, is like the first.
A third is like the former. Filthy hags!
Why do you show me this? A fourth! Start, eyes!

What, will the line stretch out to the crack of doom?
Another yet! A seventh! I'll see no more:
And yet the eighth appears, who bears a glass
Which shows me many more; and some I see
That two-fold balls and treble scepters carry:
Horrible sight! Now, I see, 'tis true;
For the blood-bolter'd Banquo smiles upon me,
And points at them for his.

Apparitions vanish

What, is this so?

FIRST WITCH

Ay, sir, all this is so: but why
Stands Macbeth thus amazedly?
Come, sisters, cheer we up his sprites,
And show the best of our delights:
I'll charm the air to give a sound,
While you perform your antic round:
That this great king may kindly say,
Our duties did his welcome pay.

Music. The witches dance and then vanish, with Hecate

MACBETH

Where are they? Gone? Let this pernicious hour
Stand aye accursed in the calendar!
Come in, without there!

Enter Lennox

LENNOX

What's your grace's will?

MACBETH

Saw you the weird sisters?

LENNOX

No, my lord.

MACBETH

Came they not by you?

LENNOX

No, indeed, my lord.

MACBETH

Infected be the air whereon they ride;
And damn'd all those that trust them! I did hear
The galloping of horse: who was't came by?

LENNOX

'Tis two or three, my lord, that bring you word
Macduff is fled to England.

MACBETH

Fled to England!

LENNOX

Ay, my good lord.

MACBETH

Time, thou anticipatest my dread exploits:
The flighty purpose never is o'ertook
Unless the deed go with it; from this moment
The very firstlings of my heart shall be
The firstlings of my hand. And even now,
To crown my thoughts with acts, be it thought and done:
The castle of Macduff I will surprise;
Seize upon Fife; give to the edge o'the sword
His wife, his babes, and all unfortunate souls
That trace him in his line. No boasting like a fool;
This deed I'll do before this purpose cool.

But no more sights!—Where are these gentlemen?
Come, bring me where they are.

Exeunt

Scene II. Fife. Macduff's castle.

Enter Lady Macduff, her Son, and Ross

LADY MACDUFF

What had he done, to make him fly the land?

ROSS

You must have patience, madam.

LADY MACDUFF

He had none:
His flight was madness: when our actions do not,
Our fears do make us traitors.

ROSS

You know not
Whether it was his wisdom or his fear.

LADY MACDUFF

Wisdom! to leave his wife, to leave his babes,
His mansion and his titles in a place
From whence himself does fly? He loves us not;
He wants the natural touch: for the poor wren,
The most diminutive of birds, will fight,
Her young ones in her nest, against the owl.
All is the fear and nothing is the love;
As little is the wisdom, where the flight
So runs against all reason.

ROSS

My dearest coz,

I pray you, school yourself: but for your husband,
He is noble, wise, judicious, and best knows
The fits o'the season. I dare not speak much further;
But cruel are the times, when we are traitors
And do not know ourselves, when we hold rumour
From what we fear, yet know not what we fear,
But float upon a wild and violent sea
Each way and move. I take my leave of you:
Shall not be long but I'll be here again:
Things at the worst will cease, or else climb upward
To what they were before. My pretty cousin,
Blessing upon you!

LADY MACDUFF

Father'd he is, and yet he's fatherless.

ROSS

I am so much a fool, should I stay longer,
It would be my disgrace and your discomfort:
I take my leave at once.

Exit

LADY MACDUFF

Sirrah, your father's dead;
And what will you do now? How will you live?

SON

As birds do, mother.

LADY MACDUFF

What, with worms and flies?

SON

With what I get, I mean; and so do they.

LADY MACDUFF

Poor bird! thou'ldst never fear the net nor lime,
The pitfall nor the gin.

SON

Why should I, mother? Poor birds they are not set for.
My father is not dead, for all your saying.

LADY MACDUFF

Yes, he is dead; how wilt thou do for a father?

SON

Nay, how will you do for a husband?

LADY MACDUFF

Why, I can buy me twenty at any market.

SON

Then you'll buy 'em to sell again.

LADY MACDUFF

Thou speak'st with all thy wit: and yet, i'faith,
With wit enough for thee.

SON

Was my father a traitor, mother?

LADY MACDUFF

Ay, that he was.

SON

What is a traitor?

LADY MACDUFF

Why, one that swears and lies.

SON

And be all traitors that do so?

LADY MACDUFF

Every one that does so is a traitor, and must be hanged.

SON

And must they all be hanged that swear and lie?

LADY MACDUFF

Every one.

SON

Who must hang them?

LADY MACDUFF

Why, the honest men.

SON

Then the liars and swearers are fools,
for there are liars and swearers enow to beat
the honest men and hang up them.

LADY MACDUFF

Now, God help thee, poor monkey!
But how wilt thou do for a father?

SON

If he were dead, you'ld weep for
him: if you would not, it were a good sign
that I should quickly have a new father.

LADY MACDUFF

Poor prattler, how thou talk'st!

Enter a Messenger

MESSENGER

Bless you, fair dame! I am not to you known,
Though in your state of honour I am perfect.
I doubt some danger does approach you nearly:
If you will take a homely man's advice,
Be not found here; hence, with your little ones.
To fright you thus, methinks, I am too savage;

To do worse to you were fell cruelty,
Which is too nigh your person. Heaven preserve you!
I dare abide no longer.

Exit

LADY MACDUFF

Whither should I fly?
I have done no harm. But I remember now
I am in this earthly world; where to do harm
Is often laudable, to do good sometime
Accounted dangerous folly: why then, alas,
Do I put up that womanly defence,
To say I have done no harm?

Enter Murderers

What are these faces?

FIRST MURDERER

Where is your husband?

LADY MACDUFF

I hope, in no place so unsanctified
Where such as thou mayst find him.

FIRST MURDERER

He's a traitor.

SON

Thou liest, thou shag-hair'd villain!

FIRST MURDERER

What, you egg!

Stabbing him

Young fry of treachery!

SON

He has kill'd me, mother:

Run away, I pray you!

Dies

Exit Lady Macduff, crying 'Murder!' Exeunt Murderers, following her

Scene III. England. Before the King's palace.

Enter Malcolm and Macduff

MALCOLM

Let us seek out some desolate shade, and there
Weep our sad bosoms empty.

MACDUFF

Let us rather
Hold fast the mortal sword, and like good men
Bestride our down-fall'n birthdom: each new morn
New widows howl, new orphans cry, new sorrows
Strike heaven on the face, that it resounds
As if it felt with Scotland and yell'd out
Like syllable of dolour.

MALCOLM

What I believe I'll wail,
What know believe, and what I can redress,
As I shall find the time to friend, I will.
What you have spoke, it may be so perchance.
This tyrant, whose sole name blisters our tongues,
Was once thought honest: you have loved him well.
He hath not touch'd you yet. I am young; but something
You may deserve of him through me, and wisdom
To offer up a weak poor innocent lamb
To appease an angry god.

MACDUFF

I am not treacherous.

MALCOLM

But Macbeth is.
A good and virtuous nature may recoil
In an imperial charge. But I shall crave your pardon;
That which you are my thoughts cannot transpose:
Angels are bright still, though the brightest fell;
Though all things foul would wear the brows of grace,
Yet grace must still look so.

MACDUFF

I have lost my hopes.

MALCOLM

Perchance even there where I did find my doubts.
Why in that rawness left you wife and child,
Those precious motives, those strong knots of love,
Without leave-taking? I pray you,
Let not my jealousies be your dishonours,
But mine own safeties. You may be rightly just,
Whatever I shall think.

MACDUFF

Bleed, bleed, poor country!
Great tyranny! lay thou thy basis sure,
For goodness dare not cheque thee: wear thou thy wrongs;
The title is affeer'd! Fare thee well, lord:
I would not be the villain that thou think'st
For the whole space that's in the tyrant's grasp,
And the rich East to boot.

MALCOLM

Be not offended:
I speak not as in absolute fear of you.
I think our country sinks beneath the yoke;
It weeps, it bleeds; and each new day a gash
Is added to her wounds: I think withal
There would be hands uplifted in my right;
And here from gracious England have I offer
Of goodly thousands: but, for all this,
When I shall tread upon the tyrant's head,
Or wear it on my sword, yet my poor country
Shall have more vices than it had before,
More suffer and more sundry ways than ever,
By him that shall succeed.

MACDUFF

What should he be?

MALCOLM

It is myself I mean: in whom I know
All the particulars of vice so grafted
That, when they shall be open'd, black Macbeth
Will seem as pure as snow, and the poor state
Esteem him as a lamb, being compared
With my confineless harms.

MACDUFF

Not in the legions
Of horrid hell can come a devil more damn'd
In evils to top Macbeth.

MALCOLM

I grant him bloody,

Luxurious, avaricious, false, deceitful,
Sudden, malicious, smacking of every sin
That has a name: but there's no bottom, none,
In my voluptuousness: your wives, your daughters,
Your matrons and your maids, could not fill up
The cistern of my lust, and my desire
All continent impediments would o'erbear
That did oppose my will: better Macbeth
Than such an one to reign.

MACDUFF

Boundless intemperance
In nature is a tyranny; it hath been
The untimely emptying of the happy throne
And fall of many kings. But fear not yet
To take upon you what is yours: you may
Convey your pleasures in a spacious plenty,
And yet seem cold, the time you may so hoodwink.
We have willing dames enough: there cannot be
That vulture in you, to devour so many
As will to greatness dedicate themselves,
Finding it so inclined.

MALCOLM

With this there grows
In my most ill-composed affection such
A stanchless avarice that, were I king,
I should cut off the nobles for their lands,
Desire his jewels and this other's house:
And my more-having would be as a sauce
To make me hunger more; that I should forge

Quarrels unjust against the good and loyal,
Destroying them for wealth.

MACDUFF

This avarice
Sticks deeper, grows with more pernicious root
Than summer-seeming lust, and it hath been
The sword of our slain kings: yet do not fear;
Scotland hath foisons to fill up your will.
Of your mere own: all these are portable,
With other graces weigh'd.

MALCOLM

But I have none: the king-becoming graces,
As justice, verity, temperance, stableness,
Bounty, perseverance, mercy, lowliness,
Devotion, patience, courage, fortitude,
I have no relish of them, but abound
In the division of each several crime,
Acting it many ways. Nay, had I power, I should
Pour the sweet milk of concord into hell,
Uproar the universal peace, confound
All unity on earth.

MACDUFF

O Scotland, Scotland!

MALCOLM

If such a one be fit to govern, speak:
I am as I have spoken.

MACDUFF

Fit to govern!
No, not to live. O nation miserable,

With an untitled tyrant bloody-scepter'd,
When shalt thou see thy wholesome days again,
Since that the truest issue of thy throne
By his own interdiction stands accursed,
And does blaspheme his breed? Thy royal father
Was a most sainted king: the queen that bore thee,
Oftener upon her knees than on her feet,
Died every day she lived. Fare thee well!
These evils thou repeat'st upon thyself
Have banish'd me from Scotland. O my breast,
Thy hope ends here!

MALCOLM

Macduff, this noble passion,
Child of integrity, hath from my soul
Wiped the black scruples, reconciled my thoughts
To thy good truth and honour. Devilish Macbeth
By many of these trains hath sought to win me
Into his power, and modest wisdom plucks me
From over-credulous haste: but God above
Deal between thee and me! for even now
I put myself to thy direction, and
Unspeak mine own detraction, here abjure
The taints and blames I laid upon myself,
For strangers to my nature. I am yet
Unknown to woman, never was forsworn,
Scarcely have coveted what was mine own,
At no time broke my faith, would not betray
The devil to his fellow and delight
No less in truth than life: my first false speaking

Was this upon myself: what I am truly,
Is thine and my poor country's to command:
Whither indeed, before thy here-approach,
Old Siward, with ten thousand warlike men,
Already at a point, was setting forth.
Now we'll together; and the chance of goodness
Be like our warranted quarrel! Why are you silent?

MACDUFF

Such welcome and unwelcome things at once
'Tis hard to reconcile.

Enter a Doctor

MALCOLM

Well; more anon.—Comes the king forth, I pray you?

DOCTOR

Ay, sir; there are a crew of wretched souls
That stay his cure: their malady convinces
The great assay of art; but at his touch—
Such sanctity hath heaven given his hand—
They presently amend.

MALCOLM

I thank you, doctor.

Exit Doctor

MACDUFF

What's the disease he means?

MALCOLM

'Tis call'd the evil:
A most miraculous work in this good king;
Which often, since my here-remain in England,
I have seen him do. How he solicits heaven,

Himself best knows: but strangely-visited people,
All swoln and ulcerous, pitiful to the eye,
The mere despair of surgery, he cures,
Hanging a golden stamp about their necks,
Put on with holy prayers: and 'tis spoken,
To the succeeding royalty he leaves
The healing benediction. With this strange virtue,
He hath a heavenly gift of prophecy,
And sundry blessings hang about his throne,
That speak him full of grace.

Enter Ross

MACDUFF

See, who comes here?

MALCOLM

My countryman; but yet I know him not.

MACDUFF

My ever-gentle cousin, welcome hither.

MALCOLM

I know him now. Good God, betimes remove
The means that makes us strangers!

ROSS

Sir, amen.

MACDUFF

Stands Scotland where it did?

ROSS

Alas, poor country!
Almost afraid to know itself. It cannot
Be call'd our mother, but our grave; where nothing,
But who knows nothing, is once seen to smile;

Where sighs and groans and shrieks that rend the air
Are made, not mark'd; where violent sorrow seems
A modern ecstasy; the dead man's knell
Is there scarce ask'd for who; and good men's lives
Expire before the flowers in their caps,
Dying or ere they sicken.

MACDUFF

O, relation
Too nice, and yet too true!

MALCOLM

What's the newest grief?

ROSS

That of an hour's age doth hiss the speaker:
Each minute teems a new one.

MACDUFF

How does my wife?

ROSS

Why, well.

MACDUFF

And all my children?

ROSS

Well too.

MACDUFF

The tyrant has not batter'd at their peace?

ROSS

No; they were well at peace when I did leave 'em.

MACDUFF

But not a niggard of your speech: how goes't?

ROSS

When I came hither to transport the tidings,
Which I have heavily borne, there ran a rumour
Of many worthy fellows that were out;
Which was to my belief witness'd the rather,
For that I saw the tyrant's power a-foot:
Now is the time of help; your eye in Scotland
Would create soldiers, make our women fight,
To doff their dire distresses.

MALCOLM

Be't their comfort
We are coming thither: gracious England hath
Lent us good Siward and ten thousand men;
An older and a better soldier none
That Christendom gives out.

ROSS

Would I could answer
This comfort with the like! But I have words
That would be howl'd out in the desert air,
Where hearing should not latch them.

MACDUFF

What concern they?
The general cause? or is it a fee-grief
Due to some single breast?

ROSS

No mind that's honest
But in it shares some woe; though the main part
Pertains to you alone.

MACDUFF

If it be mine,
Keep it not from me, quickly let me have it.

ROSS

Let not your ears despise my tongue for ever,
Which shall possess them with the heaviest sound
That ever yet they heard.

MACDUFF

Hum! I guess at it.

ROSS

Your castle is surprised; your wife and babes
Savagely slaughter'd: to relate the manner,
Were, on the quarry of these murder'd deer,
To add the death of you.

MALCOLM

Merciful heaven!
What, man! Ne'er pull your hat upon your brows;
Give sorrow words: the grief that does not speak
Whispers the o'er-fraught heart and bids it break.

MACDUFF

My children too?

ROSS

Wife, children, servants, all
That could be found.

MACDUFF

And I must be from thence!
My wife kill'd too?

ROSS

I have said.

MALCOLM

Be comforted:
Let's make us medicines of our great revenge,
To cure this deadly grief.

MACDUFF

He has no children. All my pretty ones?
Did you say all? O hell-kite! All?
What, all my pretty chickens and their dam
At one fell swoop?

MALCOLM

Dispute it like a man.

MACDUFF

I shall do so;
But I must also feel it as a man:
I cannot but remember such things were,
That were most precious to me. Did heaven look on,
And would not take their part? Sinful Macduff,
They were all struck for thee! naught that I am,
Not for their own demerits, but for mine,
Fell slaughter on their souls. Heaven rest them now!

MALCOLM

Be this the whetstone of your sword: let grief
Convert to anger; blunt not the heart, enrage it.

MACDUFF

O, I could play the woman with mine eyes
And braggart with my tongue! But, gentle heavens,
Cut short all intermission; front to front
Bring thou this fiend of Scotland and myself;
Within my sword's length set him; if he 'scape,

Heaven forgive him too!

MALCOLM

This tune goes manly.
Come, go we to the king; our power is ready;
Our lack is nothing but our leave; Macbeth
Is ripe for shaking, and the powers above
Put on their instruments. Receive what cheer you may:
The night is long that never finds the day.

Exeunt

***

ACT V

Scene I. Dunsinane. Ante-room in the castle.

Enter a Doctor of Physic and a Waiting-Gentlewoman

DOCTOR

I have two nights watched with you, but can perceive no truth in your report. When was it she last walked?

GENTLEWOMAN

Since his majesty went into the field, I have seen her rise from her bed, throw her night-gown upon her, unlock her closet, take forth paper, fold it, write upon't, read it, afterwards seal it, and again return to bed; yet all this while in a most fast sleep.

DOCTOR

A great perturbation in nature, to receive at once the benefit of sleep, and do the effects of watching! In this slumbery agitation, besides her walking and other actual performances, what, at any time, have you heard her say?

GENTLEWOMAN

That, sir, which I will not report after her.

DOCTOR

You may to me: and 'tis most meet you should.

GENTLEWOMAN

Neither to you nor any one; having no witness to confirm my speech.

Enter Lady Macbeth, with a taper

Lo you, here she comes! This is her very guise; and, upon my life, fast asleep. Observe her; stand close.

DOCTOR

How came she by that light?

GENTLEWOMAN

Why, it stood by her: she has light by her continually; 'tis her command.

DOCTOR

You see, her eyes are open.

GENTLEWOMAN

Ay, but their sense is shut.

DOCTOR

What is it she does now? Look, how she rubs her hands.

GENTLEWOMAN

It is an accustomed action with her, to seem thus washing her hands: I have known her continue in this a quarter of an hour.

LADY MACBETH

Yet here's a spot.

DOCTOR

Hark! she speaks: I will set down what comes from her, to satisfy my remembrance the more strongly.

LADY MACBETH

Out, damned spot! out, I say!—One: two: why, then, 'tis time to do't.—Hell is murky!—Fie, my lord, fie! a soldier, and afeard? What need we fear who knows it, when none can call our power to account?—Yet who would have thought the old man to have had so much blood in him.

DOCTOR

Do you mark that?

LADY MACBETH

The thane of Fife had a wife: where is she now?—What, will these hands ne'er be clean?—No more o' that, my lord, no more o'that: you mar all with this starting.

DOCTOR

Go to, go to; you have known what you should not.

GENTLEWOMAN

She has spoke what she should not, I am sure of that: heaven knows what she has known.

LADY MACBETH

Here's the smell of the blood still: all the perfumes of Arabia will not sweeten this little hand. Oh, oh, oh!

DOCTOR

What a sigh is there! The heart is sorely charged.

GENTLEWOMAN

I would not have such a heart in my bosom for the dignity of the whole body.

DOCTOR

Well, well, well—

GENTLEWOMAN

Pray God it be, sir.

DOCTOR

This disease is beyond my practise: yet I have known those which have walked in their sleep who have died holily in their beds.

LADY MACBETH

Wash your hands, put on your nightgown; look not so pale.—I tell you yet again, Banquo's buried; he cannot come out on's grave.

DOCTOR

Even so?

LADY MACBETH

To bed, to bed! there's knocking at the gate: come, come, come, come, give me your hand. What's done cannot be undone.—To bed, to bed, to bed!

Exit

DOCTOR

Will she go now to bed?

GENTLEWOMAN

Directly.

DOCTOR

Foul whisperings are abroad: unnatural deeds
Do breed unnatural troubles: infected minds

To their deaf pillows will discharge their secrets:
More needs she the divine than the physician.
God, God forgive us all! Look after her;
Remove from her the means of all annoyance,
And still keep eyes upon her. So, good night:
My mind she has mated, and amazed my sight.
I think, but dare not speak.

GENTLEWOMAN

Good night, good doctor.

Exeunt

Scene II. The country near Dunsinane.

Drum and colours. Enter Menteith, Caithness, Angus, Lennox, and Soldiers

MENTEITH

The English power is near, led on by Malcolm,
His uncle Siward and the good Macduff:
Revenges burn in them; for their dear causes
Would to the bleeding and the grim alarm
Excite the mortified man.

ANGUS

Near Birnam wood
Shall we well meet them; that way are they coming.

CAITHNESS

Who knows if Donalbain be with his brother?

LENNOX

For certain, sir, he is not: I have a file
Of all the gentry: there is Siward's son,
And many unrough youths that even now

Protest their first of manhood.

MENTEITH

What does the tyrant?

CAITHNESS

Great Dunsinane he strongly fortifies:
Some say he's mad; others that lesser hate him
Do call it valiant fury: but, for certain,
He cannot buckle his distemper'd cause
Within the belt of rule.

ANGUS

Now does he feel
His secret murders sticking on his hands;
Now minutely revolts upbraid his faith-breach;
Those he commands move only in command,
Nothing in love: now does he feel his title
Hang loose about him, like a giant's robe
Upon a dwarfish thief.

MENTEITH

Who then shall blame
His pester'd senses to recoil and start,
When all that is within him does condemn
Itself for being there?

CAITHNESS

Well, march we on,
To give obedience where 'tis truly owed:
Meet we the medicine of the sickly weal,
And with him pour we in our country's purge
Each drop of us.

LENNOX

Or so much as it needs,
To dew the sovereign flower and drown the weeds.
Make we our march towards Birnam.

Exeunt, marching

Scene III. Dunsinane. A room in the castle.

Enter Macbeth, Doctor, and Attendants

MACBETH

Bring me no more reports; let them fly all:
Till Birnam wood remove to Dunsinane,
I cannot taint with fear. What's the boy Malcolm?
Was he not born of woman? The spirits that know
All mortal consequences have pronounced me thus:
'Fear not, Macbeth; no man that's born of woman
Shall e'er have power upon thee.' Then fly, false thanes,
And mingle with the English epicures:
The mind I sway by and the heart I bear
Shall never sag with doubt nor shake with fear.

Enter a Servant

The devil damn thee black, thou cream-faced loon!
Where got'st thou that goose look?

SERVANT

There is ten thousand—

MACBETH

Geese, villain!

SERVANT

Soldiers, sir.

MACBETH

Go prick thy face, and over-red thy fear,
Thou lily-liver'd boy. What soldiers, patch?
Death of thy soul! those linen cheeks of thine
Are counsellors to fear. What soldiers, whey-face?

SERVANT

The English force, so please you.

MACBETH

Take thy face hence.

Exit Servant

Seyton!—I am sick at heart,
When I behold—Seyton, I say!—This push
Will cheer me ever, or disseat me now.
I have lived long enough: my way of life
Is fall'n into the sear, the yellow leaf;
And that which should accompany old age,
As honour, love, obedience, troops of friends,
I must not look to have; but, in their stead,
Curses, not loud but deep, mouth-honour, breath,
Which the poor heart would fain deny, and dare not. Seyton!

Enter Seyton

SEYTON

What is your gracious pleasure?

MACBETH

What news more?

SEYTON

All is confirm'd, my lord, which was reported.

MACBETH

I'll fight till from my bones my flesh be hack'd.

Give me my armour.

SEYTON

'Tis not needed yet.

MACBETH

I'll put it on.
Send out more horses; skirr the country round;
Hang those that talk of fear. Give me mine armour.
How does your patient, doctor?

DOCTOR

Not so sick, my lord,
As she is troubled with thick coming fancies,
That keep her from her rest.

MACBETH

Cure her of that.
Canst thou not minister to a mind diseased,
Pluck from the memory a rooted sorrow,
Raze out the written troubles of the brain
And with some sweet oblivious antidote
Cleanse the stuff'd bosom of that perilous stuff
Which weighs upon the heart?

DOCTOR

Therein the patient
Must minister to himself.

MACBETH

Throw physic to the dogs; I'll none of it.
Come, put mine armour on; give me my staff.
Seyton, send out. Doctor, the thanes fly from me.
Come, sir, dispatch. If thou couldst, doctor, cast
The water of my land, find her disease,

And purge it to a sound and pristine health,
I would applaud thee to the very echo,
That should applaud again.—Pull't off, I say.—
What rhubarb, cyme, or what purgative drug,
Would scour these English hence? Hear'st thou of them?

DOCTOR

Ay, my good lord; your royal preparation
Makes us hear something.

MACBETH

Bring it after me.
I will not be afraid of death and bane,
Till Birnam forest come to Dunsinane.

DOCTOR

[*Aside*] Were I from Dunsinane away and clear,
Profit again should hardly draw me here.

Exeunt

Scene IV. Country near Birnam wood.

Drum and colours. Enter Malcolm, Siward and Young Siward, Macduff, Menteith, Caithness, Angus, Lennox, Ross, and Soldiers, marching

MALCOLM

Cousins, I hope the days are near at hand
That chambers will be safe.

MENTEITH

We doubt it nothing.

SIWARD

What wood is this before us?

MENTEITH

The wood of Birnam.

MALCOLM

Let every soldier hew him down a bough
And bear't before him: thereby shall we shadow
The numbers of our host and make discovery
Err in report of us.

SOLDIERS

It shall be done.

SIWARD

We learn no other but the confident tyrant
Keeps still in Dunsinane, and will endure
Our setting down before't.

MALCOLM

'Tis his main hope:
For where there is advantage to be given,
Both more and less have given him the revolt,
And none serve with him but constrained things
Whose hearts are absent too.

MACDUFF

Let our just censures
Attend the true event, and put we on
Industrious soldiership.

SIWARD

The time approaches
That will with due decision make us know
What we shall say we have and what we owe.
Thoughts speculative their unsure hopes relate,
But certain issue strokes must arbitrate:

Towards which advance the war.

Exeunt, marching

Scene V. Dunsinane. Within the castle.

Enter Macbeth, Seyton, and Soldiers, with drum and colours

MACBETH

Hang out our banners on the outward walls;
The cry is still 'They come:' our castle's strength
Will laugh a siege to scorn: here let them lie
Till famine and the ague eat them up:
Were they not forced with those that should be ours,
We might have met them dareful, beard to beard,
And beat them backward home.

A cry of women within

What is that noise?

SEYTON

It is the cry of women, my good lord.

Exit

MACBETH

I have almost forgot the taste of fears;
The time has been, my senses would have cool'd
To hear a night-shriek; and my fell of hair
Would at a dismal treatise rouse and stir
As life were in't: I have supp'd full with horrors;
Direness, familiar to my slaughterous thoughts
Cannot once start me.

Re-enter Seyton

Wherefore was that cry?

SEYTON

The queen, my lord, is dead.

MACBETH

She should have died hereafter;
There would have been a time for such a word.
To-morrow, and to-morrow, and to-morrow,
Creeps in this petty pace from day to day
To the last syllable of recorded time,
And all our yesterdays have lighted fools
The way to dusty death. Out, out, brief candle!
Life's but a walking shadow, a poor player
That struts and frets his hour upon the stage
And then is heard no more: it is a tale
Told by an idiot, full of sound and fury,
Signifying nothing.

Enter a Messenger

Thou comest to use thy tongue; thy story quickly.

MESSENGER

Gracious my lord,
I should report that which I say I saw,
But know not how to do it.

MACBETH

Well, say, sir.

MESSENGER

As I did stand my watch upon the hill,
I look'd toward Birnam, and anon, methought,
The wood began to move.

MACBETH

Liar and slave!

MESSENGER

Let me endure your wrath, if't be not so:
Within this three mile may you see it coming;
I say, a moving grove.

MACBETH

If thou speak'st false,
Upon the next tree shalt thou hang alive,
Till famine cling thee: if thy speech be sooth,
I care not if thou dost for me as much.
I pull in resolution, and begin
To doubt the equivocation of the fiend
That lies like truth: 'Fear not, till Birnam wood
Do come to Dunsinane:' and now a wood
Comes toward Dunsinane. Arm, arm, and out!
If this which he avouches does appear,
There is nor flying hence nor tarrying here.
I gin to be aweary of the sun,
And wish the estate o'the world were now undone.
Ring the alarum-bell! Blow, wind! come, wrack!
At least we'll die with harness on our back.

Exeunt

Scene VI. Dunsinane. Before the castle.

Drum and colours. Enter Malcolm, Siward,
Macduff, and their Army, with boughs

MALCOLM

Now near enough: your leafy screens throw down.
And show like those you are. You, worthy uncle,
Shall, with my cousin, your right-noble son,

Lead our first battle: worthy Macduff and we
Shall take upon's what else remains to do,
According to our order.

SIWARD

Fare you well.
Do we but find the tyrant's power to-night,
Let us be beaten, if we cannot fight.

MACDUFF

Make all our trumpets speak; give them all breath,
Those clamorous harbingers of blood and death.

Exeunt

Scene VII. Another part of the field.

Alarums. Enter Macbeth

MACBETH

They have tied me to a stake; I cannot fly,
But, bear-like, I must fight the course. What's he
That was not born of woman? Such a one
Am I to fear, or none.

Enter Young Siward

YOUNG SIWARD

What is thy name?

MACBETH

Thou'lt be afraid to hear it.

YOUNG SIWARD

No; though thou call'st thyself a hotter name
Than any is in hell.

MACBETH

My name's Macbeth.

YOUNG SIWARD

The devil himself could not pronounce a title
More hateful to mine ear.

MACBETH

No, nor more fearful.

YOUNG SIWARD

Thou liest, abhorred tyrant; with my sword
I'll prove the lie thou speak'st.

They fight and Young Siward is slain

MACBETH

Thou wast born of woman
But swords I smile at, weapons laugh to scorn,
Brandish'd by man that's of a woman born.

Exit

Alarums. Enter Macduff

MACDUFF

That way the noise is. Tyrant, show thy face!
If thou be'st slain and with no stroke of mine,
My wife and children's ghosts will haunt me still.
I cannot strike at wretched kerns, whose arms
Are hired to bear their staves: either thou, Macbeth,
Or else my sword with an unbatter'd edge
I sheathe again undeeded. There thou shouldst be;
By this great clatter, one of greatest note
Seems bruited. Let me find him, fortune!
And more I beg not.

Exit.

Alarums. Enter Malcolm and Siward

SIWARD

This way, my lord; the castle's gently render'd:
The tyrant's people on both sides do fight;
The noble thanes do bravely in the war;
The day almost itself professes yours,
And little is to do.

MALCOLM

We have met with foes
That strike beside us.

SIWARD

Enter, sir, the castle.

Exeunt. Alarums

Scene VIII. Another part of the field.

Enter Macbeth

MACBETH

Why should I play the Roman fool, and die
On mine own sword? whiles I see lives, the gashes
Do better upon them.

Enter Macduff

MACDUFF

Turn, hell-hound, turn!

MACBETH

Of all men else I have avoided thee:
But get thee back; my soul is too much charged
With blood of thine already.

MACDUFF

I have no words:
My voice is in my sword: thou bloodier villain

Than terms can give thee out!

They fight

MACBETH

Thou losest labour:
As easy mayst thou the intrenchant air
With thy keen sword impress as make me bleed:
Let fall thy blade on vulnerable crests;
I bear a charmed life, which must not yield,
To one of woman born.

MACDUFF

Despair thy charm;
And let the angel whom thou still hast served
Tell thee, Macduff was from his mother's womb
Untimely ripp'd.

MACBETH

Accursed be that tongue that tells me so,
For it hath cow'd my better part of man!
And be these juggling fiends no more believed,
That palter with us in a double sense;
That keep the word of promise to our ear,
And break it to our hope. I'll not fight with thee.

MACDUFF

Then yield thee, coward,
And live to be the show and gaze o'the time:
We'll have thee, as our rarer monsters are,
Painted on a pole, and underwrit,
'Here may you see the tyrant.'

MACBETH

I will not yield,

To kiss the ground before young Malcolm's feet,
And to be baited with the rabble's curse.
Though Birnam wood be come to Dunsinane,
And thou opposed, being of no woman born,
Yet I will try the last. Before my body
I throw my warlike shield. Lay on, Macduff,
And damn'd be him that first cries, 'Hold, enough!'

Exeunt, fighting. Alarums

Retreat. Flourish. Enter, with drum and colours, Malcolm, Siward, Ross, the other Thanes, and Soldiers

MALCOLM

I would the friends we miss were safe arrived.

SIWARD

Some must go off: and yet, by these I see,
So great a day as this is cheaply bought.

MALCOLM

Macduff is missing, and your noble son.

ROSS

Your son, my lord, has paid a soldier's debt:
He only lived but till he was a man;
The which no sooner had his prowess confirm'd
In the unshrinking station where he fought,
But like a man he died.

SIWARD

Then he is dead?

ROSS

Ay, and brought off the field: your cause of sorrow
Must not be measured by his worth, for then
It hath no end.

SIWARD

Had he his hurts before?

ROSS

Ay, on the front.

SIWARD

Why then, God's soldier be he!
Had I as many sons as I have hairs,
I would not wish them to a fairer death:
And so, his knell is knoll'd.

MALCOLM

He's worth more sorrow,
And that I'll spend for him.

SIWARD

He's worth no more
They say he parted well, and paid his score:
And so, God be with him! Here comes newer comfort.

Re-enter Macduff, with Macbeth's head

MACDUFF

Hail, king! for so thou art: behold, where stands
The usurper's cursed head: the time is free:
I see thee compass'd with thy kingdom's pearl,
That speak my salutation in their minds;
Whose voices I desire aloud with mine:
Hail, King of Scotland!

ALL

Hail, King of Scotland!

Flourish

MALCOLM

We shall not spend a large expense of time

Before we reckon with your several loves,
And make us even with you. My thanes and kinsmen,
Henceforth be earls, the first that ever Scotland
In such an honour named. What's more to do,
Which would be planted newly with the time,
As calling home our exiled friends abroad
That fled the snares of watchful tyranny;
Producing forth the cruel ministers
Of this dead butcher and his fiend-like queen,
Who, as 'tis thought, by self and violent hands
Took off her life; this, and what needful else
That calls upon us, by the grace of Grace,
We will perform in measure, time and place:
So, thanks to all at once and to each one,
Whom we invite to see us crown'd at Scone.

Flourish. Exeunt

Commentary

Act I

Macbeth Commentary provides a comprehensive description of every act with explanations and translations for all important quotes.

Act I. Scene I.—A desert place.

Second Witch: "When the hurlyburly's done, / When the battle's lost and won."

On a heath the Three Witches decide to meet again after a battle being fought nearby. Thunder, storms and the desolate heath, paint a gloomy picture, setting the tone of this play and defining an imagery of nature at war with itself, a recurring theme in this play...

The play begins upon a heath. Thunder and lighting rake the air. Three Witches ask themselves when they shall next meet, deciding that it will be "When the hurlyburly's done, / When the battle's lost and won" (Line 4). This will be later in the day at "the set of sun" (Line 5) upon a heath again where they will meet Macbeth. Together the Three Witches cry, "Fair is foul, and foul is fair: / Hover through the fog and filthy air" (Line 13).

Act I. Scene II.—A camp near Forres.

A bleeding Sergeant: "For brave Macbeth—well he deserves that name...."

Macbeth is introduced to us as the brave man who led King Duncan's forces to victory against the traitorous Thane of Cawdor, Macdonwald and The King of Norway, in a battle that could have gone either way were it not for Macbeth's leadership. We learn that Macbeth killed Macdonwald himself in battle. King Duncan, overjoyed, decides to make Macbeth his new Thane of Cawdor. The previous Thane of Cawdor will be executed.

King Duncan, his sons Malcolm and Donalbain, and noblemen Lennox enter, meeting with a bleeding Sergeant. He speaks to the King of a battle between the King's forces and those of the traitorous Macdonwald.

Victory was not assured, but then Macbeth entered the fray, "For brave Macbeth,-well he deserves that name,—/ Disdaining fortune [ignoring the dangers], with his brandish'd steel [with his sword]... carv'd out his passage [carved his way through the battle / entered the fight]" (Lines 21-24).

Later we learn that Macbeth killed Macdonwald himself, securing his head to the King's battlements: "he unseam'd [cut him open] him from nave to the chaps, / And fix'd his head upon our battlements" (Line 28).

The Norwegian Lord however began a fresh assault, the bleeding Sergeant explains, but Macbeth and Banquo met them: "they / Doubly redoubled strokes upon the foe: [they redoubled their efforts against the enemy]" (Line 45).

The Sergeant finishes his report with praise: "They [Macbeth and Banquo] smack of honour both" (Line 51).

Nobleman Ross enters, announcing to the King and company that the King of Norway himself "With terrible numbers, / Assisted by that most disloyal traitor, / The Thane of Cawdor, began a dismal conflict;" (the King of Norway with huge numbers of men, helped by that traitorous Thane of Cawdor started a terrible battle), (Lines 61-63).

Only when Macbeth, described as the bridegroom of the goddess of war arrived, did the King's men emerge triumphant with the Norwegians now pleading for peace: "Till that Bellona's bridegroom, lapp'd in proof, / Confronted him with self-comparisons," (Lines 64-65).

We learn of King Duncan's great pleasure. "Great happiness!" (Line 69), King Duncan says on hearing that his forces have defeated the King of Norway's and that the King of Norway's dead are to buried but not before the payment of ten thousand dollars for the King's general use or rather as part of the terms of peace the defeated Norwegians have made with King Duncan.

Duncan is no longer fooled by the Thane of Cawdor's treachery and instructs Ross to "pronounce his present death, / And with his former title greet Macbeth" (Line 77).

King Duncan explains that "What he [the last Thane of Cawdor's title] hath [has] lost noble Macbeth hath won" (the title that the Thane of Cawdor has lost, Macbeth has now won], (Lines 79).

The Thane of Cawdor will be executed and Macbeth will now have the previous traitor's title.

Act I. Scene III.—A heath near Forres.

Banquo: "What! can the devil speak true?"

The Three Witches' establish their malicious nature before meeting Macbeth and Banquo. The Three Witches tell Macbeth that he will be "Thane of Glamis!", "Thane of Cawdor!" and "king hereafter", or become the King of Scotland. Banquo learns that his descendants shall be kings.

Banquo is suspicious of the Three Witches, remembering that they often trick men. Macbeth initially agrees but when

Ross and Angus tell him he has been made the new Thane of Cawdor, Macbeth in a very important aside (soliloquy), remarks, "Glamis and Thane of Cawdor: / The greatest is behind."

Macbeth now first questions Banquo on his feelings about his descendants becoming kings and then starts to think of killing King Duncan to make prophecy fact but later hopes fate alone will spare him the need to kill...

Again thunder foreshadows the Three Witches' appearance. The First Witch asks of the second's activities. We learn she has been busy "Killing swine" (Line 2). We learn a sailor's wife had chestnuts, which she denied the Second Witch.

Together they resolve to punish the women's husband. "I'll drain him dry as hay: / Sleep shall neither night nor day" the First Witch threatens (Line 20).

We hear drums. Macbeth arrives. He is with his friend Banquo. Banquo is not sure the Three Witches are actually women: "Upon her skinny lips: you should be women, / And yet your beards forbid me to interpret / That you are so" (Line 48).

Macbeth asks them to speak if they can. The First Witch addresses Macbeth as "Thane of Glamis!" (Line 50). The Second Witch pronounces Macbeth as the "Thane of Cawdor!" (Line 51) and the Third Witch as "king hereafter [ever after] " (Line 52).

Banquo asks that his future be told. The Three Witches cryptically comply: "Lesser than King Macbeth, and greater" and "Not so happy, yet much happier" ending with the line, "Thou shalt get kings, though thou be none:" (Lines 67-69).

Macbeth demands to know more...

He is already Thane (Lord) of Glamis. But how can he be The Thane of Cawdor and later King when both titles are already taken? The Three Witches vanish.

Macbeth realizes that Banquo's children will be kings, and Banquo realizes that according to the Three Witches' prophecy Macbeth will be Thane of Cawdor.

Ross and Angus arrive, informing Macbeth that he is indeed Thane of Cawdor. Banquo is amazed "What! can the devil speak true?" (What! Can the devil be trusted to tell the truth?), (Line 111).

Macbeth makes his first great soliloquy: "Glamis, and Thane of Cawdor: / The greatest is behind" (Line 123). Ross and Angus depart, leaving Macbeth and Banquo.

Macbeth darkly (and suspiciously) questions Banquo's ambitions: "Do you hope your children shall be kings, / When those [the witches] that gave the Thane of Cawdor to me / Promis'd no less to them?" (Lines 125-127).

Banquo like many of his time, fears the Three Witches: "The instruments of darkness tell us truths, / Win us with honest trifles [honest tidbits of information], to betray's / In deepest consequence. Cousins, a word, I pray you", (the instruments of darkness such as the Three Witches often tell us meaningless truths in order to later betray us most damagingly later), (Lines 132-135).

Macbeth is still confused by his good fortune: "This supernatural soliciting / Cannot be ill, cannot be good; if ill, / Why hath [has] it given me earnest of success, / Commencing in a truth? I am Thane of Cawdor:" (this advise from the Three Witches cannot be evil but it cannot be good either. Why has it given me reason to believe it by predicting my new title?), (Lines 139-142).

In an important turning point for Macbeth, he now starts to have murderous thoughts:

If good, why do I yield [give in] to that suggestion [idea of murdering King Duncan] / Whose horrid image doth [does] unfix my hair [make me sick] / And make my seated heart knock at my ribs, / Against the use of nature? Present fears / Are less than horrible imaginings; / My thought, whose murder yet is but fantastical, / Shakes so my single state of man that function / Is smother'd in surmise, and nothing is / But what is not (Lines 143-151)

Macbeth hopes in an aside (private speech revealing Macbeth's thoughts to the audience) that fate not murder, may bring him his kingdom instead: "If chance will have me king, why, chance may crown me, / Without my stir [without me doing anything about it]" (Line 154). Macbeth and Banquo resolve to see the King.

Act I. Scene IV.—Forres. The palace.

Macbeth: "Stars, hid your fires! Let not light see my black and deep desires...."

Macbeth meets King Duncan, thanking him for his new title (The Thane of Cawdor). The also loyal Banquo receives nothing. King Duncan remarks how he completely trusted the previous Thane of Cawdor. King Duncan announces that his son, Malcolm will be the new Prince of Cumberland. Macbeth sees Malcolm as a threat to what he now takes seriously as his destiny to become King of Scotland, a major turning point in Macbeth's changing morality. Macbeth makes this clear by famously asking in an aside (private speech), for the stars to hide their fires least they reveal his dark and deadly purpose or intent to kill King Duncan.

King Duncan at his castle asks of the fate of the traitorous Thane of Cawdor. Malcolm explains that the previous Thane of Cawdor did confess his treason and that he died "As one that had been studied in his death / To throw away the dearest thing he ow'd, / As 'twere a careless trifle [as if his life was unimportant]" (Line 12).

Ominously and in view of Macbeth's future betrayal, ironically, Duncan exclaims one can't tell a person's character by their face adding that the previous Thane of Cawdor was a gentleman upon which the King "built / An absolute trust" (a man King Duncan trusted completely), (Line 16).

Next Macbeth, Banquo, Ross and Angus enter. Macbeth humbly explains in thanks that what he did for the King is nothing more than that of a loyal subject: "The service and the loyalty I owe, / In doing it, pays itself" (Line 26).

Banquo too is loyal but receives no title nor thanks. King Duncan announces that his son Malcolm is to be made the Prince of Cumberland.

In an aside (soliloquy), Macbeth ends the scene already plotting his way to kingdom: "The Prince of Cumberland! that is a step / On which I must fall down, or else o'er-leap [leap over / remove], / For in my way it lies" (Line 57).

Macbeth already sees Duncan's son as an obstacle to his destiny. Ominously, Macbeth adds "Stars, hid your fires! Let not light see my black and deep desires;" (Line 58).

Duncan will soon arrive at Macbeth's castle.

Act I. Scene V.—Inverness. Macbeth's castle.

Lady Macbeth: "Come, you spirits / That tend on mortal thoughts! unsex me here, / And fill me from the crown to the toe full / Of direst cruelty: make thick my blood, / Stop up the access and passage to remorse...."

Lady Macbeth learns by letter from Macbeth of the Three Witches' prophecies for her husband and eagerly embraces them as fact. Fearing Macbeth is too compassionate and weak-willed to do what needs to be done (killing King Duncan), she famously asks the gods to remove from her all signs of compassion and femininity, replacing them with cold remorseless ruthlessness.

Learning from a messenger that King Duncan will stay at their castle, she enthusiastically greets this news, suggesting that she already has plans to kill King Duncan. Macbeth and Lady Macbeth decide to speak again on the issue of the prophecies, Macbeth still uncertain of the need to kill King Duncan.

At Macbeth's castle we meet Lady Macbeth who is reading a letter. We learn that she knows of Macbeth's meeting with the

Three Witches. Immediately, Lady Macbeth accepts the prophecy as fact.

No doubts like Banquo, Lady Macbeth enthusiatically says: "Glamis thou art, and Cawdor; and shalt be / What thou [you] art [were] promis'd" (Line 16).

She fears Macbeth is too good to seek what he is his by destiny: "Yet do I fear thy [Macbeth's] nature; / It is too full o' [of] the milk of human kindness / To catch the nearest way [to do what needs to be done];" (Line 18).

Lady Macbeth wishes to use her powers of persuasion to prevent Macbeth denying them his destiny: "And chastise with the valour of my tongue / All that impedes thee from the golden round," (Line 27).

She learns from a messenger that King Duncan will soon arrive. Pleased, she immediately makes plans saying the messenger has announced or "croaks [announces] the fatal entrance of Duncan / Under my battlements into my castle]" (Line 43).

She famously calls upon the spirits to rid her of all her good: "Come, you spirits / That tend on mortal thoughts! unsex me here, / And fill me from the crown to the toe [head to toe]top full / Of direst cruelty: make thick my blood, / Stop up the access and passage to remorse," (Lines 44-48).

Macbeth arrives and Lady Macbeth already tells Macbeth to appear innocent like a flower but to be "the serpent under't" (Line 74). She advises him to entrust the evening to her care and exclaims that King Duncan will not see tomorrow. Macbeth says they will speak further on the issue.

Act I. Scene VI.—Before Macbeth's castle.

At Macbeth's castle King Duncan arrives whilst Lady Macbeth plays the most perfect of hostesses. Macbeth's castle seems to be a haven of snactuary, so much so that Banquo describes it as being almost heaven like in its peacefulness. King Duncan asks "Where's the Thane of Cawdor?" who is not yet present (Line 24).

Act I. Scene VII.—Macbeth's castle.

Macbeth: "False face must hide what false heart doth know."

A guilt-ridden Macbeth wrestles with his conscience, certain that he should not kill King Duncan yet guiltily having to remind himself of all the reasons why it would be wrong. Macbeth decides against murdering his King but Lady Macbeth belittles him for not being able to murder, threatening to take away her love for him if he does not. This threat wins Macbeth over and Lady Macbeth outlines her plan to kill King Duncan in his sleep while he is a guest at their castle.

The scene begins with Macbeth in his castle. Macbeth is wrestling with his conscience. Can he kill a King who is in his trust as a guest in his home?

He's here in double trust: / First, as I am his kinsman and his subject, / Strong [strong reasons] both against the deed [killing King Duncan]; then, as his host, / Who should against his murderer shut the door, / Not bear the knife myself.

(King Duncan is here in double trust. First because I am his kinsman and a subject of his, I have two very good reasons not to murder my King. Then as his host I should be shutting the door on King Duncan's murderers not holding the knife against him myself), (Lines 12-16).

Additionally King Duncan has been so good a King that "his virtues / Will plead like angels trumpet-tongu'd against / The deep damnation of his taking-off [dying];" (Line 18-20). Furthermore, Macbeth argues that he has no reason to kill his king but to satisfy "Vaulting ambition, which o'er-leaps [overleaps] itself / And falls on the other."

Macbeth will not kill his King... Lady Macbeth enters and upon learning this, scolds him as being less than a man. Additionally Lady

Macbeth makes an ultimatum: "From this time / Such I account thy love" (from now on or what you now do will I measure your love for me), (Line 42).

She argues that Macbeth was a man when he discussed this "enterprise" with her (Line 53). Finally she informs him that she would have "dash'd the brains out," (Line 63) of her own children had she "so sworn as you [Macbeth]" to the act of murdering King Duncan (Line 63).

Macbeth is worried of the consequences should they fail. Lady Macbeth outlines the plan to kill King Duncan in his sleep reassuring him that this will be easy.

Macbeth and wife will approach the sleeping King and perform their deed.

Afterwards, Lady Macbeth explains, the King's two guards will be smeared with blood implicating them: "Will it not be receiv'd, / When we have mark'd with blood those sleepy two / Of his own chamber and us'd their very daggers, / That they have done't?" (will it not be believed that these two men who sleep with the King and will have been smeared with blood will be accused of murdering the King with their own daggers?), (Line 85).

Macbeth ends this scene, decided on the murderous task ahead of him: "False face must hide what false heart doth [does] know" (Line 92).

Act II

Act II. Scene I.—Court of Macbeth's castle.

Macbeth: "Is this a dagger which I see before me...."

Banquo and son Fleance arrive at Macbeth's castle. Banquo is troubled by the Three Witches' prophecy and tells Macbeth this. Macbeth pretends not to take the Three Witches seriously. Learning from Banquo that King Duncan

is asleep, Macbeth, alone, follows an imaginary dagger to King Duncan's bedchamber where he will kill him in his sleep...

Banquo and son Fleance are walking in the castle preceded by a servant bearing a torch. Fleance exclaims, "Hold [stop], take my sword. There's husbandry in heaven; / Their candles are all out" (Line 5). Fleance can't sleep, so troubled is he by his own thoughts: "A heavy summons lies like lead upon me, / And yet I would not sleep: merciful powers!" (Line 8).

Banquo suspects the presence of danger but can not say exactly what it is. Macbeth meets them and when the question "Who's there?" is asked, replies "A friend" (Lines 12-13).

Banquo is surprised Macbeth is not yet asleep and informs Macbeth that the King is asleep having been in "unusual pleasure," (been unusually happy), (Line 15). So pleased is the King with Lady Macbeth's hospitality that a diamond has been given to the generous host (Lady Macbeth).

Cryptically, Banquo mentions a dream he had of "the three weird sisters [The Three Witches]:" to Macbeth.

Macbeth replies that "I think not of them:" (Line 26). Macbeth does however want to discuss the Three Witches with Banquo in the future.

Macbeth now alone, sees a dagger, asking himself, "Is this a dagger which I see before me," which later sports "goats of blood," or becomes covered in blood before his eyes (Lines 41).

He worries again and upon hearing a bell ring (Lady Macbeth's signal) proceeds towards King Duncan's chambers: "Hear it not [the bell], Duncan; for it is a knell [calling] / That summons thee [you, King Duncan] to heaven or to hell" (Line 71).

Act II. Scene II.—The same.

Macbeth: "Will all great Neptune's ocean wash this blood / Clean from my hand?"

Lady Macbeth has drugged King Duncan's guards, allowing Macbeth to kill King Duncan unchallenged. Lady Macbeth was to have killed the King but his resemblance to her late father means Macbeth does the deed instead. A bell frightens Lady Macbeth and Macbeth too is nervous, but he announces that he did indeed kill King Duncan.

Macbeth recounts that the two guards cried out "'Murder'" and later "'God bless us!'", Lady Macbeth telling her husband not to fret over such things and the fact that his conscience prevented him from saying "'Amen,'" when they said "'God bless us!'" Lady Macbeth tells her husband a little water will wash away their guilt and the two retire to their bedroom when knocking is later heard...

Lady Macbeth enters, remarking that the alcohol that has made the guards drunk has made her bold: "That which hath [has] made them drunk hath made me bold," (Line 1). She has drugged King Duncan's two guards. Macbeth enters and Lady Macbeth fears a bell which has sounded (Line 4) may have awakened the two guards without the murder having taken place.

We learn that Lady Macbeth was to have killed the King but the King's resemblance to her father stopped her. Macbeth announces that he has "done the deed" (Line 17) and asking if she heard, she replies only that she heard an owl scream and a cricket cry.

Macbeth was nervous and when two men in the adjoining room cried, "'Murder!'" and later "'God bless us!'" (Lines 29-34), Macbeth could not reply "'Amen,'" (Lines 34-36) as the other man did, variously interpreted as symbolic of the fact that Macbeth no longer sees himself as connected to God or on the side of good.

Macbeth thought he heard a voice say "'Sleep no more! / 'Macbeth does murder sleep,' the innocent sleep...", "'Glamis hath [has] murder'd sleep, and therefore Cawdor [Macbeth] / Shall sleep no more, Macbeth shall sleep no more!'" (Lines 44-53).

Lady Macbeth tells Macbeth not to think such things and to get some water to wash away the blood.

Lady Macbeth scolds Macbeth for bringing the daggers with him, telling him to return them to the scene of the crime. He won't and scolding Macbeth as "Infirm of purpose!" (Line 64) or weak-willed, she returns the daggers smearing blood on the grooms faces to implicate them.

Macbeth wonders if water is enough to clear his conscience: "Will all great Neptune's ocean wash this blood / Clean from my hand?" (Line 74).

Both Macbeth and his wife hear knocking.

Lady Macbeth suggests that they retire to their chamber, saying "A little water clears us of this deed;" (Line 81).

Act II. Scene III.—The same.

Donalbain: "There's daggers in men's smiles: the near in blood, / The nearer bloody."

Macduff and Lennox, the source of the knocking in the last scene, arrive at Macbeth's castle. News of King Duncan's death reaches all at Macbeth's castle. Lady Macbeth faints and Macbeth in rage kills the two drunken guards after claiming that they obviously killed their King. These actions largely free Macbeth and Lady Macbeth from suspicion. King Duncan's sons, Malcolm and Donalbain are introduced, both men wisely deciding to flee Macbeth's castle as a precaution against their own murder. Malcolm will head for England, Donalbain for Ireland.

At the castle gates we hear knocking. The Porter attending the door exclaims that he is akin to the porter of hell and we soon learn that the earlier knocking was caused by the arrival of Macduff and Lennox, Macduff engaging the Porter in some insightful yet trivial banter (Lines 25-48).

Macduff and Lennox enter and are shortly greeted by Macbeth. Macduff asks of the King. Macbeth leads Macduff to the King's chambers.

Shortly afterwards, we hear from Macduff, "O horror! horror! horror! Tongue nor heart / Cannot conceive nor name thee!" (Line 79).

Macbeth asks what the problem is, and feigning surprise incredulously asks if the King's life is what he speaks of. Macbeth and Lennox awaken the rest of the castle.

Lady Macbeth asks what's going on, Banquo tells Lady Macbeth who later feints.

Macbeth says that had he died before this deed, he would have "liv'd [lived] a blessed time; for, from this instant, / There's nothing serious in mortality," (Lines 114-115).

Malcolm and Donalbain hear of their father's death from Banquo and Macbeth exclaims that he killed the two bridegrooms in his fury.

The two brothers wisely conclude that their lives are now in danger, Malcolm decides to head for England, Donalbain for Ireland.

Donalbain famously exclaims "There's daggers in men's smiles: the near in blood, / The nearer bloody" (Lines 173-174).

Act II. Scene IV.—Outside Macbeth's castle.

Ross speaks with an Old Man who describes various unnatural acts happening in Scotland, perhaps the single most significant scene for the theme of nature at war with itself, which relates to the idea of a natural order being disturbed by killing a King, a prevalent theme throughout this play.

We learn that King Duncan's two sons have fled, leaving Macbeth to be crowned the new King of Scotland. Macduff, who later becomes instrumental in Macbeth's downfall, has

significantly snubbed Macbeth's coronation at Scone to go instead to Fife. A tone of increasing despair for Scotland begins in this scene...

Ross speaks to an Old Man who discusses nature at war with itself.

The Old Man speaks of a falcon killed by an owl last Tuesday and Ross adds that King Duncan's horses "Turn'd wild in nature, broke their stalls, flung out," (Lines 18), the Old Man remarking that "'Tis [it is] said they eat each other" (Line 21).

Macduff arrives, commenting that King Duncan's two sons have run away "which puts upon them / Suspicion of the deed" (which puts on them the suspicion that they killed their father, King Duncan), (Line 33).

Ross does not accept this explanation; why would the two sons kill their own father whom he refers to as their "own life's means!" or someone they depend upon, adding that such an action is "'Gainst nature still!" or unnatural (Lines 34-36). Ross now remarks that the kingdom will most likely reside with Macbeth and tellingly, we learn that Macduff will head to Fife and not to Scone where Macbeth will be crowned King.

The Old Man ends Act II, remarking "That would make good of bad, and friends of foes!" (Line 51).

Act III

Act III. Scene I.—Forres. The palace.

Macbeth: "Our fears in Banquo / Stick deep, and in his royalty of nature / Reigns that which would be fear'd: 'tis much he dares... Whose being I do fear; and under him / My genius is rebuk'd, as it is said / Mark Antony's was by Caesar."

Banquo is fearful that the Three Witches' prophecies are coming true, questioning whether Macbeth played most foully for it, or killed King Duncan to make prophecy, fact.

Meeting with Macbeth, Macbeth continuously asks Banquo of his travel plans and those of his son. Alone, Macbeth fears that Banquo's sons will mean his dynasty will be short-lived; only he will be King and not his sons who will be replaced by those of Banquo's lineage. Macbeth arranges for several murderers to discreetly kill Banquo and Fleance to ensure his sons and not Banquo's become future kings...

The scene begins with Banquo, alone, suspicious of Macbeth and the Three Witches' prophecy:

"Thou [you, Macbeth] hast [has] it now: King, Cawdor, Glamis, all, / As the weird women promis'd; and, I fear, / Thou [Macbeth] play'dst [played] most foully for't [for it];" (Line 1).

Banquo wonders about the prophecies made to him: "But that myself should be the root and father / Of many kings… May they not be my oracles as well, / And set me up in hope? But, hush! no more" (Lines 5-10).

Macbeth invites Banquo to a feast at his castle and obliquely (indirectly) asks his plans for the evening. "Ride you this afternoon?" (Line 21) Macbeth ominously asks. Macbeth tells us that "our bloody cousins are bestow'd / In England and Ireland, not confessing / Their cruel parricide [murdering a father, King Duncan]," (Line 35). This is a reference to King Duncan's two sons being in hiding.

Macbeth asks again of Banquo's travel plans, specifically for his son: "Goes Fleance with you?" (Line 39). Macbeth is now alone with an Attendant. He asks of some men. We learn they are presently waiting outside the palace gate. "Bring them before us" Macbeth commands. (Line 50).

Macbeth now alone, reveals his innermost thoughts in another aside: "Our fears in Banquo / Stick deep, and in his royalty of nature / Reigns that which would be fear'd: 'tis much he dares... Whose being I do fear; and under him / My genius is rebuk'd, as it is said / Mark Antony's was by Caesar" (Lines 52-60).

Macbeth goes on to remark that the Three Witches have "plac'd a fruitless crown, / And put a barren sceptre" (Line 65) in Macbeth's possession. Without a line of kings following Macbeth's line, he fears that being King of Scotland is a farce and in Banquo, Macbeth sees the person stopping his own lineage of kings.

Macbeth is interrupted by the murderers whom he instructs to kill Banquo and son Fleance. He explains to them that their problems are the result of Banquo. Taunting them, he asks them if they are happy to let the source of their pain off so easily. They reply that they are "men," (Line 97).

Macbeth tells the men to do their deed covertly (secretly) to protect Macbeth's reputation. The scene ends with Macbeth resolute of his next murder: "It is concluded [decided]: Banquo, thy [your] soul's flight, If it find heaven, must find it out to-night" (Banquo, you will die tonight to find out if your soul will go to heaven or not tonight), (Line 154).

Act III. Scene II.—The palace.

Lady Macbeth and Macbeth speak in private. Macbeth is again plagued by a guilt we thought may have vanished: "We have scotch'd the snake, not kill'd it..." (Line 15). Lady Macbeth attempts to strengthen Macbeth's resolve.

Act III. Scene III.—A park near the palace.

The Three Murderers kill Banquo but his son Fleance escapes and survives. The Three Witches' prophecy of Banquo's sons becoming kings has not been thwarted by Macbeth...

The Third Murderer joins the previous two we know of. When asked who sent him, the Third replies "Macbeth" (Line 2). The Second tells the Third not to distrust Macbeth, he delivers and can be trusted. The Third hears horses.

The Third Murderer adds Banquo's horses have stopped some way from the castle; it is common practice to walk to the castle itself. Banquo and Fleance approach the murderers by torch.

The Three Murderers set upon Banquo. Banquo cries "O, treachery! Fly, good Fleance, fly, fly, fly!" (O, treachery! Run Fleance, run, run, run!), (Line 25). Banquo dies, Fleance escapes. The Three Murderers notice this and decide to report "how much is done" (Line 32).

Act III. Scene IV.—The same. Hall in the palace.

"I am in blood / Stepp'd in so far, that, should I wade no more, / Returning were as tedious as go o'er."

Macbeth and a lady are entertaining at their castle. The First Murderer arrives, announcing that Banquo is dead but Fleance has lived. Macbeth immediately realizes the consequences of this (his descendants may not become kings). Macbeth sees Banquo's Ghost at his party, causing Lady Macbeth to finish their party early to prevent further suspicions about Macbeth's sanity and about their role in recent events (King Duncan's death whilst a guest at their castle). Macbeth makes his famous quote about being too covered in blood to stop...

A banquet is prepared attended by Macbeth, his lady, Ross, Lennox, Lords and some Attendants. Macbeth intends to play host: "Ourself will mingle with society / And play the humble host" (Line 4). Lady Macbeth echoes this sentiment: "Pronounce it for me, sir, to all our friends; / For my heart speaks they are welcome" (Line 9).

The First Murderer enters, informing Macbeth of the deed. He informs Macbeth that "Fleance is 'scaped" (Fleance escaped), (Line 23). Macbeth asks about Banquo to which the First Murderer replies that Banquo is safe: "Ay, my good lord; safe in a ditch he bides, / With twenty trenched gashes on his head;" (Line 30).

Macbeth is all too aware of the consequences of Fleance's escape: "There the grown serpent lies: the worm that's fled / Hath [has] nature that in time will venom breed," (Fleance the worm that escaped will in time breed a venom or line of kings Macbeth was hoping to prevent), (Line 33).

Macbeth whilst eating, is haunted by the Ghost of Banquo. Macbeth's talking to himself begins to unsettle Lady Macbeth. She fears Macbeth may say something suspicious and so she ends the feast early (Line 122).

Macbeth now reveals that he knows Macduff's movements; "I keep a servant fee'd" (Line 155) or has spies to keep him informed of his enemies. Macbeth, still shaken by Banquo's Ghost resolves to see the Three Witches or "the weird sisters:" tomorrow, since Macbeth is eager for reassurance and to know more of his destiny.

Macbeth now famously utters his expression that he has killed so many and is so covered in blood that he can now metaphorically speaking, no longer turn back and seek salvation:

I am in blood / Stepp'd in so far, that, should I wade no more, / Returning were as tedious as go o'er"

(Literal translation: I am in blood so deeply stepped that even if I waded or walked no more, returning would be as tedious or as time consuming and difficult as going over or returning), (Line 161).

Says Lady Macbeth, "You lack the season of all natures, sleep" (Line 164).

Act III. Scene V.—A Heath.

Hecate: "you all know security / Is mortals' chiefest enemy."

Hecate, clearly in a position of command over the Three Witches, scolds her subordinates for helping an unappreciative Macbeth. Hecate instructs the Three Witches to make preparations for her plan to use illusion and the Three Witches' prophecies against Macbeth. The Three Witches,

eager to placate their master, eagerly make preparations, doing as they are told...

Again to the prelude of thunder we see the Three Witches. They meet with Hecate, which has been interpreted as the Lord of the Witches but whose exact relationship to the Three Witches is never made explicit. All that we do know is that the Three Witches fear and respect Hecate, doing as she instructs them.

Hecate is angry with her charges. They have meddled with Macbeth without her consultation. She mocks them for helping a man who "Loves for his own ends, not for you" (loves or cares only about himself, not the Three Witches), (Line 13).

Hecate tells the Three Witches too "make amends now:" telling them to leave and meet her "at the pit of Acheron", the name for Hell's river the next morning (Lines 14-15).

By the end of the scene Hecate gains the Three Witches' support for her plan. Her plan is to use illusion to "draw him [Macbeth] on to his confusion:" (Line 29).

Macbeth will then "spurn [ignore] fate, scorn death, and bear / His hopes 'bove [above] wisdom, grace, and fear; / And you all know security / Is mortals' chiefest enemy" (ignore fate, mock or scorn death, become arrogant, take his own opinions above wisdom, grace and fear and you all know that complacency or false security is a person's worst enemy), (Line 33).

The scene ends with the First Witch suggesting haste with their preparations. After all Hecate will "soon be back again" (Line 36).

Act III. Scene VI.—Forres. The palace.

We see Lennox and a Lord discuss affairs in their kingdom. Lennox points out that all those who have sided with Macbeth, namely the late King Duncan, "the right-valiant Banquo" (Line 5) have paid dearly for this decision. Lennox slyly suggests that Fleance may be responsible for Banquo's death since he fled afterwards but we quickly realize this is Lennox's way of finding out the Lord's allegiances.

Lennox discusses how terrible it was that Donalbain and Malcolm killed their father King Duncan. Macbeth certainly did grieve... He adds that should Fleance, Donalbain and Malcolm be captured that they would certainly suffer but now Lennox realizing just how dangerous his skeptical words of Macbeth are, changes the subject by asking of Macduff.

We learn from the Lord who now makes his disgust of Macbeth quite clear that an army is being formed in England to fight Macbeth. "The son of Duncan" Malcolm is now at the English court and has been well received by the "most pious Edward" (Line 28). We finally learn that Macbeth knows this and is preparing for possible war. Macduff may be in great danger...

Act IV

Act IV. Scene I.—A cavern. In the middle, a boiling cauldron.

The First Apparition: "Beware Macduff; Beware the Thane of Fife."

The Second Apparition: "none of women born Shall harm Macbeth."

The Third Apparition: "be lion-mettled, proud, and take no care who chafes, who frets… until Great Birnam wood to high Dunsinane Hill /Shall come against him [Macbeth]."

A major turning point in the play. Just as the Three Witches' prophesied Macbeth's ascendancy to become King in Act I, Scene III, here they prophesies his doom with Three Apparitions (visions / ghosts).

The First Apparition tells an eager Macbeth that he should fear Macduff, saying "beware Macduff; / Beware the Thane of Fife...." The Second Apparition reassures Macbeth that "none of women born / Shall harm Macbeth" and the

Third Apparition tells Macbeth he has nothing to fear until "Great Birnam wood" moves to "high Dunsinane hill" near his castle.

Macbeth decides to kill Macduff to protect himself and takes the prophecies to mean he is safe from all men since they are all born naturally and that only the moving of a nearby forest to his castle, an unlikely event will spell his doom.

Next Macbeth demands to know about Banquo's descendants, learning to his anger that they will still rule Scotland rather than Macbeth's descendants. Macbeth learns that he cannot kill Macduff so instead has his entire family murdered...

The Three Witches add various ingredients to a brew in a cauldron. Together the Three Witches chant: "Double, double, toil and trouble; / Fire burn and cauldron bubble" (Lines 10-11). The Second Witch adds: "Fillet and fenny snake, / In the cauldron boil and bake;" (Line 13). Hecate enters, congratulating the Three Witches on their good work.

Macbeth arrives, rudely demanding to know his fate: "How now, you secret, black, and mid-night hags!" (Line 48).

Macbeth doesn't care about the consequences of his inquires: "Even till destruction sicken; answer me / To what I ask you" (Line 62).

The Three Witches are more than willing and forthcoming to answer Macbeth, the First Witch telling Macbeth to "Speak" the Second Witch telling Macbeth to "Demand" and the Third Witch assuring Macbeth that "We'll answer" (Lines 63, 64-65).

When offered the option of hearing from the Three Witches' masters, Macbeth eagerly agrees: "Call 'em: let me see 'em" (Line 68).

Three Apparitions (ghosts / visions) follow one at a time.

The First Apparition is of an armed head. It tells Macbeth to fear Macduff: "Macbeth! Macbeth! Macbeth! beware Macduff; /

Beware the Thane of Fife. Dismiss me. Enough" (Lines 78-79). Macbeth however will not let the First Apparition leave, but it leaves nonetheless.

The Second Apparition arrives, replacing the First Apparition... This is in the form of a "bloody Child."

It advises Macbeth to "Be bloody, bold and resolute; laugh to scorn / The power of man, for none of women born / Shall harm Macbeth" (be bloody, bold and decisive. Laugh at the power of man since no man of natural birth shall ever harm Macbeth), (Line 88).

Macbeth decides to kill Macduff anyway to be "double sure, / And take a bond of fate:" (to be on the safe side), (Line 91).

The Third Apparition is of a "Child crowned, with a tree in his hand." It tells Macbeth to "Be lion-mettled, proud, and take no care / Who chafes, who frets... until Great Birnam wood to high Dunsinane hill / Shall come against him" (be strong like a Lion, proud and do not care who chafes or resists or conspires against you until Great Birnam wood, a nearby forest moves to Dunsinane Hill) comes toward him (Line 103).

Macbeth is relieved since he has nothing to fear until a forest nearby, decides to move upon Macbeth's castle at Dunsinane hill, an event Macbeth quite naturally considers quite unlikely if not impossible; woods don't move nor walk...

Macbeth wants to know more and so asks one last question: "shall Banquo's issue [children] ever / Reign in this kingdom?" (Line 102). The Three Witches tell him to "Seek to know no more" (do not ask), (Line 113).

Arrogantly Macbeth replies, "deny me this, / And an eternal curse fall on you!" (Line 116). The Three Witches oblige, showing Macbeth a show of kings, eight in fact, the last with a glass in his hand, Banquo's Ghost following.

Macbeth is not pleased to see this: "Thou art to like the spirit of Banquo; down!" (you look too much like Banquo; down!), "Thy crown does sear mine eyeballs:" (Your crown hurts my eyes), (Line 124).

Macbeth now insults these kings (Lines 113-122) describing them all as a "Horrible sight!" (Line 133).

The Three Witches leave followed by Hecate, and Lennox enters. Macbeth interrogates Lennox on whether he saw the Three Witches; he answers that he did not. We learn from Lennox that Macduff "is fled to England" (has run off to England), (Line 157).

Macbeth decides that "from this moment / The very firstlings of my heart shall be / The firstlings of my hand" (Line 164). He will surprise Macduff's castle or "Seize upon Fife;" (Line 167) and "give to the edge of the sword / His [Macduff's] wife, his babes [children], and all unfortunate souls / That trace him in his line [those that follow Macduff]" (Line 169).

Since Macbeth cannot kill Macduff, he will destroy all vestiges (traces) of him instead.

Act IV. Scene II.—Fife. Macduff's castle.

Lady Macduff is greeted by Ross, Lady Macduff expressing her anger at being abandoned by Macduff for little reason when in her eyes, Macduff has done nothing requiring him to flee. Ross leaves and after Lady Macduff tells her son that his father is dead and a traitor, a Messenger warns Lady Macduff to flee but Macbeth's murderers succeed in killing her son. The scene ends with Lady Macduff fleeing for her life...

We find Macduff's family alone, serene and as the audience is all too aware, in mortal danger. Lady Macduff is not happy despite the advice of Ross to have patience, Lady Macduff explaining that "His [Macduff's] flight [escape] was madness: when our actions do not, / Our fears do make us traitors" (Line 5).

Lady Macduff laments that her husband "Loves us not;" (Line 10)

Ross leaves and Lady Macduff speaks with her son.

Lady Macduff tells her son that his father, Macduff is "dead:" wondering how her son will now fend for himself without a father? The son replies that he will live "As birds do, mother", Lady Macduff wondering if this means her son will feed on worms and flies and laments that this will be the future for her child (Line 36).

She explains to her son that his father was a traitor explaining that a traitor is one who "swears and lies" (Line 52).

The son defends Macduff's name when a Messenger arrives warning them all to "Be not found here;" (Do not be here), (Line 72). The Messenger leaves daring not to stay a moment longer (Line 76).

Lady Macduff though warned to flee, says that she has "done no harm" (done nothing wrong), (Line 78).

The Murderers arrive, Lady Macduff refusing to tell them Macduff's whereabouts. The Murderers call Macduff a "traitor" (Line 88).

Macduff's son calls the Murderers liars and is then stabbed exclaiming "He has killed me, mother: / Run away I pray you!" (Line 93). The scene ends with Lady Macduff being pursued by the Murderers.

Act IV. Scene III.—England. Before the King's palace.

Macduff: "Fit to govern! No, not to live."

Malcolm and Macduff discuss how Scotland under Macbeth's rule has been plunged into despair. Malcolm tests Macduff's integrity by describing himself as unfit to rule. After Malcolm disgusts Macduff with increasingly sordid descriptions of his lust and greed, Macduff tells Malcolm he is not fit to rule. This delights Malcolm who explains that he was lying; he described himself so negatively to test Macduff's integrity. We learn that a large army is gathering to defeat Macbeth.

Malcolm and Macduff speak of the sad fate of Scotland, Malcolm suggesting that they should "Weep our sad bosoms empty" at the fate of their Scotland (Line 2).

Malcolm evokes Macbeth's name as evil: "This tyrant, whose sole name blisters our tongues, / Was once thought honest: you have lov'd him well;" (Line 15) whilst Macduff expresses his despair for Scotland by saying "I have lost my hopes" (Line 28).

Malcolm asks Macduff why he left his family: "Why in that rawness left your wife and child—/ Those precious motives, those strong knots of love—/ Without leave-taking?" (Line 32).

Macduff replies "Bleed, bleed, poor country! Great tyranny, lay thou thy basis sure, / For goodness dares not cheek thee!" (Line 38).

Malcolm also fears for Scotland:

I think our country sinks beneath the yoke; / It weeps, it bleeds, and each new day a gash / Is added to her wounds... And here from gracious England have I offer / Of goodly thousands: but, for all this, / When I shall tread upon the tyrant's head, / Or wear it on my sword, yet my poor country / Shall have more vices [problems] than it had before, / More suffer [suffering], and more sundry ways than ever, / By him that shall succeed.

(Our country Scotland suffers a new wound each day. Here in England I fortunately have the help of thousands of men on offer to help reclaim Scotland yet even when I have stepped on Macbeth's head or carried it on my sword my country will have more problems and more suffering for the man who then leads it than before), (Lines 45-55)

Macduff is surprised by this last sentence. Under whom could Scotland suffer more than Macbeth? Malcolm replies "It is myself I mean;" (Line 57).

From this point, Malcolm describes himself in ever greater terms of evil, Malcolm advising Macduff to "Esteem [judge] him [Macbeth] as a lamb," compared to him (Line 61).

Malcolm declares that he is voluptuous, liking scores of women, greedy, and lacks all of "the king-becoming graces," that he should have (Line 103).

After hearing all this Macduff tells Malcolm he is not only not fit to govern but unfit to live as well: "Fit to govern! No, not to live" (Line 117).

Malcolm is pleased that Macduff has the integrity to say this. He explains that his descriptions were a lie adding that he is in fact a virgin or "Unknown to woman," and that "my first false speaking / Was this upon myself" (Line 146) or that Malcolm was earlier not telling the truth, and that "Old Siward, with ten thousand war-like men, / Already at a point," (Line 150) are setting forth for Scotland but now that Malcolm knows Macduff to be honorable, they will set forth together.

Macduff is a little confused: "'Tis hard to reconcile" (this is hard to fathom), (Line 154).

A Doctor speaks with Malcolm discussing an illness (Lines 156-160) later described by Malcolm as evil. Malcolm confirms the Doctor's early statements that the King of England merely by his presence (163-172), appears to cure the sick, Malcolm describing The King of England's effect on the sick as a "strange virtue," (Line 173).

Ross arrives but Malcolm does not know him, saying of him, "My countryman; but yet I know him not" (Line 178).

Ross tells them more about Scotland:

Alas! Poor country; / Almost afraid to know itself. It cannot / Be call'd our mother, but our grave; where nothing, / But who knows nothing, is once seen to smile; / Where sighs and groans and shrieks that rent [fill] the air / Are made, not mark'd; where violent sorrow seems / A modern ecstasy.... (Lines 184-190)

We learn after some delay from Ross that Macduff's family have been murdered (Line 237).

Malcolm is distraught, "Merciful heaven! What! man; ne'er [never] pull your hat upon your brows; / Give sorrow words; the grief that does not speak / Whispers the o'er-fraught heart and bids it break" (Lines 239-208).

Macduff asks of his children: "My children too?" (Line 243). Ross replies "Wife, children, servants, all / That could be found" (Line 244).

Malcolm, acting very much like a King should, leading and lifting his men's spirits, suggests Macduff use his sorrow to productive use: "Be comforted: / Let's make us medicine of our great revenge, / To cure this deadly grief" (Line 251).

Macduff points out however that whatever he does to Macbeth, "He [Macbeth] has no children" so Macduff's revenge can never be total; Macbeth will never suffer the loss of losing a child or in Macduff's case, children (Line 252).

Still in shock, Macduff asks "What! all my pretty chickens and their dam / At one fell swoop? (Line 255), (have I lost them all) to which Malcolm replies, "Dispute it like a man" (Line 256).

Macduff swears revenge: "But, gentle heavens, / Cut short all intermission; front to front / Bring thou this fiend of Scotland [Macbeth] and myself; / Within my sword's length set him; if he 'scape, / Heaven forgive him too!" (but gentle heavens, do not take waste any more time. Bring Macbeth within a sword's length of me and if he escapes, heaven forgive him too!), (Lines 268-272).

Malcolm ends the scene on a dark note, remarking: "The night is long that never finds the day" (Line 278).

Act V

Act V. Scene I.—Dunsinane. Ante-room in the castle.

Lady Macbeth: "Out, damned spot! out, I say! One; two: why, then, 'tis time to do't. Hell is murky!"

Lady Macbeth's insanity becomes clear... First her doctor and a nurse discuss Lady Macbeth's sleepwalking and talking to herself and then we, the audience see this for ourselves. Lady Macbeth makes her famous speech that she cannot wipe away the blood on her hands, indicating her battle to suppress her guilty conscience has failed completely...

This scene begins with a Doctor conversing with a Waiting-Gentle-woman (nurse). We learn that Lady Macbeth has been sleepwalking, uttering words the Gentlewomen is reluctant to discuss with the Doctor.

Lady Macbeth enters and we see her sleepwalking for ourselves. She is rubbing her hands and we learn this can go on for a quarter of an hour.

Lady Macbeth is distressed, famously saying: "Out, damned spot! out, I say! One; two: why, then, 'tis [it is] time to do't [do it]. Hell is murky!" (Line 32).

Lady Macbeth refers to her counterpart, Lady Macduff: "The Thane of Fife had a wife: where is she now? What! Will these hands ne'er [never] be clean? No more o'[of] that, my lord, no more o' that: you mar all with this starting" (Line 38).

She laments the permanency of her disturbance, "Here's the smell of the blood still: all the perfumes of Arabia will not sweeten this little hand. Oh! oh! oh!" (Line 45). The Doctor explains that "This disease is beyond my practice:" (this disease is beyond my abilities), (Line 52).

Lady Macbeth continues her sleep talking echoing earlier events, "To bed, to bed: there's knocking at the gate. Come, come, come, come, give me your hand. What's done cannot be undone. To bed, to bed, to bed" (Line 59).

Act V. Scene II.—The country near Dunsinane.

Macbeth's enemies gather near his castle at Dunsinane as Macbeth strongly fortifies its defenses. We learn that Macbeth's hold on Scotland is less than absolute...

Menteith, Caithness, Angus, Lennox and Soldiers are all gathered near Macbeth's castle at Dunsinane hill. Menteith explains that "The English power is near, led on by Malcolm, / His uncle Siward, and the good Macduff" (Line 1).

We learn that "Revenges burn in them;" (Line 3). Menteith has little love for Macbeth, asking "What does the tyrant?" We learn from Caithness that "Great Dunsinane he [Macbeth] strongly fortifies. Some say he's mad; others that lesser hate him / Do call it valiant fury; but, for certain, / He cannot buckle his distemper'd cause / Within the belt of rule" (Line 18).

We discover from Angus that Macbeth's title, far from be secure, is said to "Hang loose about him, like a giant's robe / Upon a dwarfish thief" (Line 25). Macbeth is clearly being described metaphorically as a man in borrowed robes too large for him like the rule of Scotland.

Act V. Scene III.—Dunsinane. A room in the castle.

Macbeth: "Bring me no more reports; let them fly all: / Till Birnam wood remove to Dunsinane / I cannot taint with fear."

Macbeth prepares to defiantly fight his enemies armed with the prophecy that he will only be defeated when the nearby "Birnam wood" moves on his castle. Macbeth learns of the ten thousand strong army against him. Seyton confirms this bad news and Macbeth donning his armor, prepares to fight his enemies recalling the "Birnam wood" prophecy once more as a source of comfort...

Macbeth is receiving reports of the English army; he is not concerned and seeks solace in the prophecy, saying "Bring me no more reports; let them fly all: Till Birnam wood remove to Dunsinane / I cannot taint with fear. What's the boy Malcolm? Was he not born of women?" (Line 1).

A Servant informs Macbeth that the army numbers ten thousand. Macbeth doesn't believe it asking if he means ten thousand "Geese, villain?" (Line 14).

Learning from the Servant that there are ten thousand soldiers against him, Macbeth resigns himself to his fate, "As honour, love, obedience, troops of friends, / I must look to have; but, in their stead, / Curses, not loud but deep, mouth-honour, breath, / Which poor heart would fain deny, and dare not" (Line 31).

Seyton confirms the reports and Macbeth instructs him to "Hang those that talk of fear: Give me mine [my] armour" (Line 40). The Doctor enters and we learn from him that "therein the patient [Lady Macbeth] / Must minister to himself" though strictly speaking the Doctor should have said "herself" (Line 53).

Macbeth appeals to the Doctor to try and help his wife and Macbeth ends this scene exclaiming, "I will not be afraid of death and bane / Till Birnam forest come to Dunsinane" (Line 67).

Act V. Scene IV.—Country near Birnam wood.

With his troops loyally around him, Malcolm orders each man to cut down a branch from the nearby Birnam Wood as his army now camouflaged under an umbrella of "Birnam wood", heads towards Macbeth's castle at Dunsinane.

Again with drum and colours, we see Malcolm, Old Siward and son, Macduff, Menteith, Caithness, Angus, Lennox, Ross and Soldiers marching. Malcolm rallies his troops, "Cousins, I hope the days are near at hand / That chambers will be safe" (Line 1). The men supportive of Malcolm, reply, "We doubt it nothing" (Line 3).

Malcolm instructs every soldier to now "hew him down a bough / And bear't before him: thereby shall we shadow / The numbers of our host, and make discovery / Err in report of us" (cut down some wood or leafy branches and carry it so we will hide our true numbers from the enemy and when discovered cause them to make mistakes in reporting us), (Line 9).

The scene ends with troops marching toward Dunsinane where Siward announces "We learn no other but the confident tyrant / Keeps still in Dunsinane," (we have heard nothing but that the tyrant Macbeth remains still in his castle at Dunsinane), (Line 12).

We also learn from Malcolm that those still fighting on Macbeth's side are merely "constrained things [people] / Whose hearts are absent too" or whose hearts are not in defending Macbeth but rather defend the tyrant under pressure, not devotion (Line 18).

Act V. Scene V.—Dunsinane. Within the castle.

Macbeth: "Life's but a walking shadow, a poor player / That struts and frets his hour upon the stage, / And then is heard no more; it is a tale / Told by an idiot, full of sound and fury, / Signifying nothing."

Macbeth laughs off his enemies' numbers, certain of the "Birnam wood" prophecy and equally certain that his fortifications should laugh off any attack. We hear a women's cry later learning that Lady Macbeth is dead. Macbeth coldly shrugs off the news that his once "dearest chuck," is dead with complete apathy. Macbeth learns that Birnam Wood or rather Malcolm's forces are moving on his castle. Realizing what this means, Macbeth nonetheless defiantly sets off to meet his destiny...

Macbeth and Seyton enter with colours or flags flying. Macbeth instructs Seyton to hang banners on the outside walls, confident that he can outlast any siege since, "Our castle's strength / Will laugh a siege to scorn; here let them lie / Till famine and the ague eat them up;" (Line 4).

We hear a cry of a woman. Macbeth asks what it is to which Seyton replies, "It is the cry of women, my good lord" (Line 9).

Macbeth answers that he has "almost forgot the taste of fears", adding "I have supp'd full [eaten full / I am full] with horrors; / Direness, familiar to my slaughterous thoughts, / Cannot once start me" (Lines 10-16).

Seyton returns, telling Macbeth "The queen, my lord, is dead" (Line 18).

Macbeth coldly replies that "She should have died hereafter; / There would have been a time for such a word" (Line 20).

Macbeth famously bids his wife farewell and likening life to an actor on stage, describes life as a fleeting experience signifying nothing:

Out, out, brief candle! Life's but a walking shadow, a poor player / That struts and frets his hour upon the stage, / And then is heard no more; it is a tale / Told by an idiot, full of sound and fury, / Signifying nothing. (Line 30)

A Messenger reports that he saw the wood begin to move. Macbeth, enraged at this apparent impossibility replies, "If thou speak'st false, / Upon the next tree shalt thou hang alive, / Till famine cling thee;" (if you are lying, upon the next tree will you hang alive until famine kills you), (Line 45).

Macbeth repeats the Birnam wood prophecy; sees this very fact and panics, "Arm, arm, and out!" (Line 51), "Ring the alarum-bell! Blow, wind! come, wrack! At least we'll die with harness on our back" (Line 56).

Act V. Scene VI.—Dunsinane. Before the castle.

Malcolm's men drop their leafy camouflage and the battle begins...

Malcolm and company are near Macbeth's castle. Malcolm instructs his men to drop their "leavy screens... And show like those you are [reveal yourselves for the soldiers you are]" (Line 2).

Malcolm tells his men where they shall attack, "You worthy uncle, / Shall, with my cousin, your right-noble son, / Lead our first battle;" (Line 4).

Macduff ends the scene on a note of optimism: "Make all our trumpets speak; give them all breath, / Those clamorous harbingers of blood and death" (Line 11).

Act V. Scene VII.—Another part of the field.

Macduff: "Turn, hell-hound, turn!"

Macbeth fights, Siward killing him. Macbeth is now confronted by Macduff, a man he has consciously avoided and one he refuses to fight. Macbeth famously exclaims that he has lived a charmed life and is unable to be killed by a man, naturally born. Macduff now explains that he has born by Caesarian section and the two men fight, Macbeth dying and order being restored when Malcolm is hailed as the new King of Scotland...

Macbeth can no longer run, "They have tied me to a stake; I cannot fly [escape / run], / But bear-like I must fight the course. What's he / That was not born of women? Such a one / Am I to fear, or none" (Malcolm and his troops have surrounded me or tied me to a stake. I cannot escape but like a bear must fight my enemies. But who is not born by a woman. Only such a person should I fear), (Line 1).

Siward enters and asks who Macbeth is. Upon learning the fact he replies, "The devil himself could not pronounce [say] a title / More hateful to mine [my] ear" (Line 10).

Macbeth responds "No, nor more fearful" (Line 12).

Macbeth kills Young Siward. Encouraged by his triumph, Macbeth gloats: "Thou wast born of women: / But swords I smile at, weapons laugh to scorn, / Brandish'd by man that's of a women born" (you were born from a woman. But swords I smile at, weapons I laugh at in scorn carried by men who are woman born), (Line 15).

Macduff enters, exclaiming that "My wife and children's ghosts will haunt me still" (Line 20). Malcolm and Old Siward begin to enter the Macbeth's castle (Line 24).

Act V. Scene VIII.—Another part of the field.

Macbeth reenters and finally as prophecy warned, Macduff and Macbeth meet. "Turn, hell-hound, turn!" Macduff shouts at Macbeth (Line 4).

Macbeth and Macduff exchange threats; Macbeth explaining that "I bear a charmed life, which must not yield / To one of women born" (I live a lucky or charmed life which cannot yield or fall to one born from a woman), (Line 15).

Macduff explains to Macbeth that he may "Despair thy charm;" (despair at his charm), (Line 17) since Macduff was "from his mother's womb / Untimely ripp'd" (born of Caesarian section or untimely ripped from his mother thus not being naturally born), (Line 20).

Macbeth, worried says that "I'll not fight with thee" (I will not fight with you), (Line 26). Macduff argues otherwise telling him to surrender so that he may be placed on a pole as an illustration of a tyrant.

Macduff explains that Macbeth's near future will involve his head being "Painted [planted] upon a pole, and underwrit," or written underneath will be the lines, "'Here may you see the tyrant [Macbeth].'" The two men fight.

With colours, Malcolm, Old Siward, Ross and Thanes and Soldiers reenter and we learn "Macduff is missing," (Line 43). Old Siward learns that he lost his son proudly exclaiming though sad, "God's soldier be he!" (Line 54). Macduff returns with Macbeth's head. All hail Malcolm as the new King of Scotland.